The Rocky Horror Picture Show

Series Editor: Barry Monush

The Rocky Horror Picture Show

Dave Thompson

AN IMPRINT OF HAL LEONARD CORPORATION

Published in 2012 by Limelight Editions
An Imprint of Hal Leonard Corporation
7777 West Bluemound Road
Milwaukee, WI 53213

Trade Book Division Editorial Offices
33 Plymouth St., Montclair, NJ 07042

Printed in the United States of America

Book design by Mark Lerner

Library of Congress Cataloging-in-Publication Data

Thompson, Dave, 1960 Jan. 3-
  The Rocky horror picture show / Dave Thompson.
     p. cm.
  Includes bibliographical references and index.
  ISBN 978-0-87910-387-3 (pbk.)
  1. O'Brien, Richard, 1942- Rocky Horror show. 2. Rocky Horror picture show (Motion picture) I. Title.
  ML410.O17T56 2012
  791.43'72--dc23

                            2012010105

www.limelighteditions.com

CONTENTS

INTRODUCTION

It's a scene that plays out every night across America, and across a large chunk of the rest of the world too. A tiny and probably downtrodden movie theater in a back street somewhere clings to life with a handful of screens where others might boast dozens, and lures in the locals not with the glitz and blitz of the modern moviegoing experience (hard seats, handkerchief screens, overpriced popcorn, and so on and so forth) but with a chance to remember a time when going to the movies was fun: the days when the décor was flash and the usherettes smiled, and the ice cream lady carried a tray around her neck.

The days when you went to the movies because you wanted to, not because you'd been bludgeoned into submission by wall-to-wall advertising.

The days when you took a chance on an unknown and it changed your life, rather than sitting through the blockbusters because nothing changed at all.

And the days when you didn't just shrug and say you'd wait for something to come out on DVD, because there were no DVDs, or home video rentals either. You saw a movie when the movie house screened it; then you waited for them to screen it again. And if sufficient people demanded it, the movie might come around again next year. Or next month. Or next week.

The Rocky Horror Picture Show comes around every week.

The Rocky Horror Picture Show is a phenomenon like no other movie before or since. We all, perhaps, can name a film that ranks among our personal favorites—a cinematic touchstone that affects us on every level that celluloid is capable of reaching, be it emotional, physical, psychological, sexual, or spiritual.

It might be a weepie, from the days before *Titanic* so devalued that concept that now everyone expects a film to make them tear up. It might be a western, redolent with symbolism, gunsmoke, and horseflesh. An action pic, a sci-fi epic . . . entire universes of imagination have sprung up around the *Star Wars* franchise, and doesn't that indicate just how our perception of the medium has changed—the fact that we could even dream of describing a series of interconnected movies as a "franchise," as though each was simply another arm of some Main Street megachain, rented out to the highest bidder to run more or less as they choose?

The Rocky Horror Picture Show is not a franchise.

Or maybe it is. There are certainly enough manifestations of it out there for fans to hoard, from the original London stage show cast album through to the latest almost-forty-years-on revival download; from the movie soundtrack to the karaoke instrumental set; from the book of the film to the book you now hold; and on to all the officially licensed geegaws and baubles that allow the most mediocre mortal to walk the walk and talk the talk of the world's most eligible Transylvanian bachelor without leaving his own pad.

Except it isn't the passing fast-buck entrepreneur who operates the offshoots from the parent company. It is everybody who lines up outside the movie house on that aforementioned Saturday night, their costumes clean and perfect, their lines well rehearsed and spot on cue, their props in hand and their moves in place. *The Rocky Horror Picture Show* may not have been shot with anything more high-tech than the industry standard cameras and mikes of the day. But it remains the world's first and finest interactive multimedia experience, a virtual world before virtual reality was dreamed of, lived out on a worldwide web that predated the Internet by almost two decades. (And no, you cannot even escape from it in the Second Life Virtual World . . . the costumes are available there as well.)

Rocky Horror is all of these things, and everything else you could want it to be. And to think, it all came from Denton High.

∽

For ease of reference, and because any discussion of the phenomenon that is Rocky Horror *cannot divorce the stage show,* The Rocky Horror Show *(or, more recently,* Richard O'Brien's Rocky Horror Show*), from the movie* The Rocky Horror Picture Show, *the term* Rocky Horror *is used throughout this book. The only exceptions are when either the movie or the stage show is being discussed specifically.*

The Rocky Horror Picture Show

CHAPTER 1

It Came from Outer Space

Rocky Horror has endured for one reason: because there is nothing else like it.

Other movies have ascended to the ranks of absolute cultdom, movies that range from the lowest 1950s B flick to the biggest budget *Star Wars*-style story—and there is a massive parallel there, because *Star Wars* too has its devoted legions who dress, speak, and even live in the manner of their onscreen idols.

But *Rocky Horror* is unique because really, does anyone know what it is? Or what it's about?

It has a story line, and that story is linear . . . it is scripted and scored, it has a beginning and end. And a middle, and that's important because, for some reason, a lot of movies forget to have anything of substance at their core.

Trying to dissect that substance, however, is another matter entirely. On the one hand, *Rocky Horror* is a simple slice of sci-fi horror, a story of aliens, sex, and rock 'n' roll, shot through with comedy, tragedy, and a heaping slice of hubris. And cannibalism. And death.

Except that the rock 'n' roll is largely irrelevant, the sex is largely twisted, and the aliens look like you or me, only with a slightly more developed dress sense. And stranger hair.

On the other hand, though—is it an allegory? Is it a commentary? Is it a warning?

Or is it just a movie that a lot of people like for a lot of different reasons, and should be allowed to keep its secrets to itself, while the rest of us just sit back and enjoy it?

"I set out to write amusing entertainment," *Rocky Horror*'s author, Richard O'Brien, explained in 1999, "so I think what I did was touch buttons that were deeper rooted. I think Mr Carl Jung might have had something to say about *Rocky* and [gotten] into the scenario of that, and pull[ed] it apart, and deconstruct[ed] it and look[ed] at the symbolism and look[ed] at the psychological motives that were within the piece.

"Of course, none of that was intended. So I think what happened was that my subconscious wrote a starchy show and I invested in it so that it's also other people's subconscious. I locked into the kind of bigger consciousness somehow and touched areas that people [had] thought about and kept hidden and hadn't really expressed. *Rocky* somehow or other releases that. But any good fairy tale sort of does that, truthfully."

So is that what it is? A fairy tale?

O'Brien thinks so. "I truly believe that *Rocky* is an eternal fairy tale. It's unpretentious. It's rock and roll. People have a good laugh. It's a bit naughty. It's got the old British smutty *Carry On* humor in it. It's easy. It's not academic. It's not rocket science. It appeals not only on a conscious level but *Rocky* resonates on a subconscious level as well.

"That's why it really works. If it just skimmed the surface, then people would go home and forget about it, but there's that subliminal level as well. It's not recognized. Look at a fairy tale and there's not much to it, but there is still this undercurrent to this tale. Inside this tale, we're talking about puberty and the journey from childhood into adulthood. *Rocky*'s exactly like that. A rite of passage. A journey. Brad and Janet are basically Hansel and Gretel, and Frank-N-Furter is the wicked witch. That's its true longevity. It's not just pantomime and nonsense; it has this unspoken depth which makes it deeply appealing."

Appealing and adored. And so often emulated that it is possible to see echoes of *Rocky Horror* every place we look—from the similar rite of passage presaged by movies as distant as *Star Wars* and *Harry Potter* to the ease with which great swathes of what *Rocky Horror* regarded as humorous asides have become assimilated into popular culture itself. Thus, although so many other movies have spawned their own devoted cohorts of living, breathing acolytes, it was *Rocky Horror* that birthed that trend, two years before *Star Wars* was more than a bunch of unedited rushes, and it is *Rocky Horror* to which cultural, societal, and even sexual psychologists find themselves returning again and again when discussing the impact that cinema *can* have on its audience.

They rarely answer the questions that their discussions ask, however—or if they do, they rarely answer them to any kind of consensus. Why is *Rocky Horror* so popular? How long is a piece of string? Why do so many people identify with it? How long does it take to fill a bathtub?

From its uncertain beginnings to the modern phenomenon, the cult of *Rocky Horror* exists for the same reason that every other cult truly takes root: because there is no single explanation for it; because everybody who is a part of that cult—and there are now several million people who have seen the film, watched the stage show, sung the songs, and/or worn the clothes—comes to it for reasons that are uniquely their own, and the beauty of *Rocky Horror* is that the concept itself allows for that.

There are rules, but there are no laws. There are conventions, but there are also *un*conventions. Nothing is set, everything is fluid, even within the tightest strictures of the traditions that govern the average viewing.

As fans (but that is too weak a word for what *Rocky Horror* audiences become . . . as *participants*) we know what to shout when, what to throw at whom, and when to bow down to another player's part. But we also know what those words and actions mean to us, and every soul can tell a different story.

Where else, after all, can the straightest dude on the block parade guilelessly in corset, suspenders, and suggestive lisp, while his girlfriend dons tap shoes and squeaks devotion to a dead biker?

Meet Frank-N-Furter, our host, and Columbia, a groupie.

Where else can a sweet maiden experiencing her first taste of love be greeted with a room full of voyeurs screaming "slut" in her face, while her bumbling boyfriend betrays his cherry to the lascivious jaws of a towering transsexual?

Meet the white-as-snow Janet Weiss, and her science nerd fiancé Brad.

Where else can a balding humpback and a French maid seductress blast their employer with a sci-fi laser gun, as he is carried *King Kong* style up the RKO radio mast by a

Charles Atlas–style Frankenstein, while a wheelchair-bound government agent does the cancan in his lingerie?

Meet Riff Raff, Magenta, Rocky, and Dr. Scott.

Where else does the evening's meal sing before it becomes supper?

Meet Eddie . . . a rocker.

And where else can the names of Joan Jett, Jonathan King, Gary Glitter, Freddie Mercury, and Meat Loaf be spoken in the same breath as those of Fay Wray, Michael Rennie, Claude Rains, and Janette Scott, without either speaker or listener even missing a beat?

The Rocky Horror Show answers all of these questions, because it was *The Rocky Horror Show* that asked them in the first place. And before anybody wonders whether they even needed to be asked in the first place, consider this. The movie simply picked up where the stage show left off, and when 2013 dawns on *Rocky*'s fortieth birthday and lazy headline writers coin fresh clichés from it doing the time warp again, the miracle will not be that *The Rocky Horror Show* has sustained itself for so long. It will be that anybody ever doubted it could.

On June 19, 1973, in a tiny, sixty-three-seat theater on London's King's Road, the world caught its first glimpse of the madness that would become *Rocky Horror*. And of the madness that would reinvent British theater . . . and, in particular, British rock-musical theater . . . for a still reasonably new decade.

Not that that was much of a challenge.

A sickly child throughout the 1950s and 1960s, when theater's only concessions to the energies of rock 'n' roll music revolved around slapping a handful of ballads into any passing stage show, the infant genre so far had been of a distinctly religious bent. Wildly successful they may have been, but *Jesus Christ Superstar*, *Godspell*, and *Joseph and the Amazing Technicolor Dreamcoat* were nevertheless wholesomely uplifting productions that all took their lead from the notion that God's only son possibly enjoyed a bit of a cavort.

There was the hippie love-in *Hair*, of course, and that raised eyebrows as well as temperatures with its unabashed affection for the sundry alternative lifestyles that were circulating around the late 1960s West; it was, we were told in earnest sing-song, the dawning of the Age of Aquarius, and free love was just one of the myriad temptations that awaited us once the sun rose. And, of course, there was The Who's "rock opera" *Tommy*, itself destined to become both a stage show and a movie; already the template for a host of future rocking conceits; and, in its own way, a smart example of the wheel turning full circle in the madly messianic moods of its titular hero.

But there was a problem. It didn't matter how hip these other productions claimed to be, or how many future legends of British rock were birthed or baptized in the musicians' pit at the plays. Even the most kindly observer was unable to see them as much more than an attempt to shoehorn rock 'n' roll energies into boxes that had hitherto been associated with sundry other arts—legitimate theater and opera, to name but two—as though to prove to an older generation that yeah, pop music's okay.

It worked well, at least to an extent. Andrew Lloyd Webber and Tim Rice, composers of *Jesus Christ Superstar*, would (individually and collectively) go on to create some of the best loved stage shows of the late twentieth century—*Evita, Chess, Cats,* and more—and all would employ the energies of rock 'n' roll to some extent. And today, rock and the theater are so firmly twinned that it is difficult to believe there was ever a time when slapping a few electric guitars over the traditional sounds of the orchestra pit was even considered mildly controversial.

But there was always a disconnect; always a sense of one genre only flirting with the energies of another; always a need for the *yin* to find its *yang*, without knowing where to look.

And then *The Rocky Horror Show* came along, with its cast of corset-clad transvestite aliens, Frankensteinian muscle men, innocent college kids, a squealing groupie, and a fabulous array of punch-above-their-weight rock 'n' roll songs, and it altered the landscape forever.

And why? Because it didn't actually pay any attention to the landscape, just drove across it regardless.

It has been said, on many occasions, that *The Rocky Horror Show* was simply a child of its times—the height of the British music industry's obsession with glam rock, the musical fandango that thrust David Bowie, Marc Bolan, Roxy Music, and a host of other glitter-clad devils to the commercial forefront. But it was also their parent.

Its musical parameters notwithstanding, glam rock had just three fixations: sex, in as many varieties as could be found; science fiction, with as kitsch an angle as could be schemed; and a yearning nostalgia for the 1950s, when everything was simpler and tasted better too. *Rocky Horror* seized upon those same ingredients, inflated them beyond parody, and, in so doing, reminded us why we fell in love with them all to begin with. In the words of the song, "Don't dream it, be it."

Richard Hartley, musical director of both the *Rocky Horror* stage show and the movie, explained, "It was at the time that the sexual liberation permeated. The glam rock thing, that just happened, too. All those elements . . . just the right collection of people in the right place at the right time." And he was correct.

Not necessarily among the right people, but certainly in the right place at the right time, Gary Weightman was thirteen the first time he saw *The Rocky Horror Show*, catching the billboard outside the Classic every time he rode the number eleven bus up the King's Road in Chelsea, and growing more and more curious with every fresh sighting.

It was a striking image, after all.

"I was a huge David Bowie fan, Lou Reed, Marc Bolan, the whole glam rock thing, and every time I saw the sign or read another mention of the play in one of the music papers, the more convinced I was that it was something I needed to see. But I also knew, or suspected, that it was something that I maybe *didn't* want to see—at thirteen, your feelings about sex and sexuality are still very much up in the air, and *Rocky Horror* was pure sex, that much was obvious, and probably very twisted sex.

"Plus, I'd never been to the theater before, and it was still a time when doing that was a very 'grown up' thing to do, so there was an extra sense of stepping into an unknown world. But I put aside some pocket money for a few weeks and then one afternoon on my way to visit my gran . . . who lived about half a mile from the theater . . . I got off the bus early, paid for my ticket and . . ."

And entered a world that sent an adolescent's eggshell mind reeling.

A note to the majority of the people reading this book: we are adults today, and *The Rocky Horror Show* is so much a part of our cultural furniture that it is impossible to see it now through the cultural prism within which it once existed.

We see it as a whole; a ninety-something-minute time span in which the events tumble in preordained sequence. We know when to laugh, when to hiss, when to throw popcorn at the screen. We have forgotten—and, depending upon when we first experienced *Rocky Horror*, may never even have known—just how powerful those images were when they first manifested on the London stage: how shocking that first glimpse of Frank-N-Furter; how bizarre his plans for poor Rocky; how vertiginous his seduction of both Brad and Janet.

Particularly Janet. Actress Jessica Harper, who played an older and, perhaps, less naïve Janet Weiss in 1981's *Shock Treatment*, reasoned, "Janet is definitely Little Miss Middle-Class. She's lived her whole life in a kind of little frilly doll house, and Brad is the ideal mate for her. In the first movie, Janet was loyal to Brad but also interested in exploring the bizarre world of Transylvania that she and Brad stumbled upon. She discovers that she really is a naughty girl."

Rocky Horror was a comedy and it was a musical. No question about that. But in the same way that a young mind would have been shocked by David Bowie's use of the English slang word (for masturbation) "wanking" in the lyrics to "Time" in that same momentous year of 1973; or by the realization of what Lou Reed was really talking about when he sang about "giving head" in that same year's "Walk on the Wild Side," *The Rocky Horror Show* took those mundane qualifications—"just" a comedy, "just" a musical—and turned them on their heads.

The Rocky Horror Show was sedition. It was debauchery. It was delirium.

"I came out of the theater at the end of the play and the whole world looked different to me," Weightman continues. "It looked drab, colorless, and gray. I felt that I'd just spent an hour and a half literally being transported into a whole new way of living and thinking, a universe in which anything was possible but, more than that, anything was *probable*. You just had to open your mind and look for it." Laughing, he confesses that one song from the show—one line, in fact—still hurtles him back in time to that cold London evening, almost forty autumns ago. Once again, it is "Don't dream it . . . be it."

The Rocky Horror Show was about three months old and already the must-see hip hit of the year when Weightman caught it. The first award, Play of the Year from the *Evening News*, fell into its grasp at the end of 1973; more accolades would follow. Most of the musical heavy-hitters of the age were sighted at the play's performances, some on more than one occasion. Many admitted both privately and publicly than the characterizations they saw on the stage reminded them . . . maybe not of themselves, but at least of their peers. That's how powerful it was.

More than a decade after he played the heavily made-up lieutenant to David Bowie's Ziggy Stardust space invader, guitarist Mick Ronson admitted that the first time he saw *The Rocky Horror Show*, he wondered why anyone else even bothered trying to be glam rock any longer, so accurately had *Rocky Horror* encapsulated its appeal; Brian Connolly, front man with the Sweet, went so far as to describe it as "the *Spinal Tap* of the 1970s.

"*Rocky Horror* took everything that was going on in glam rock, the drag, the fifties, the science fiction, and took them to ridiculous extremes." But whereas a future generation of artists would complain that *Spinal Tap* was just too close to the truth to ever be construed as amusing, Connolly admitted that he loved *Rocky Horror*—"and if I'd had the nerve, I'd have played Frank-N-Furter myself."

He was not alone in that desire. Fellow glam icon Gary Glitter went one step further and actually took on the role in earnest, touring New Zealand with a production of the play in 1977. He had *not* seen it before; he'd managed to miss the play in London and the movie in the theater before the offer came his way. So one night in Paris in 1976, he joined the line for a late-night performance, and he fell in love in the same way, and for the same reasons, as so many others are drawn to the production.

"I found a crowd of punks and freaks waiting to go in—I'd never seen anything like this . . . and began to get interested. It was what went on inside that decided me, though, as I watched the audience shouting out the words of the different characters they were identifying with. I thought this whole participation thing was so rock 'n' roll that I had to do it."

In other words, a lot of plays and movies have *tried* to capture the spirit of rock. But *Rocky Horror* just went out there and did it.

Perhaps the greatest homage of all, however, was that undertaken by Freddie Mercury, the so superbly flamboyant front man with the rock band Queen. Never afraid to flaunt his sexual predilections before an audience that lapped up every gyration, Mercury took it upon himself to become the living embodiment of Frank-N-Furter, not only utilizing elements of his dress in his stagewear but also aping his mannerisms, diction, and speech.

Neither was it a passing or limited passion. To the end of his life (Mercury passed away in 1991), the persona was not only developed but also enlarged, until Mercury himself became larger than life, and the prototype he'd seen on that tiny stage in London was, if not forgotten, at least unspoken.

Not everybody approved. Journalist Barney Hoskyns, outlining the history of the glam rock movement in the book *Glam! Bowie, Bolan and the Glitter Rock Revolution*, spoke scathingly of "Tim Curry's Frank-N-Furter pouting 'Sweet Transvestite' . . . dilut[ing] the original outrage" of the glam movement; and quoted fellow neophytes Phil Dellio and Scott Woods in condemning *Rocky Horror* for dealing glam "a serious blow by trying to satirize something that was partly conceived as satire in the first place."

Yet that argument does not hold water. Glam rock as a musical movement did not seize more than the fringes of mainstream attention until late 1972, even early 1973, by which time the seeds from which *Rocky Horror* sprang had long since germinated. Rather than parodying glam rock, then, *Rocky Horror* developed in tandem with it, tapping into the same undercurrents of sexual discovery that were fascinating so many of the genre's other musical heroes—the fact that homosexuality had been decriminalized in the UK just five years before; that government censorship of the British theater had been repealed even more recently than that.

The decision, in 1968, to strip the Lord Chamberlain's office of its 231-year-old right to vet and censor any play or production destined for a public stage remains a watershed in the history of British theater, all the more so since it was the culmination of a decade-long campaign that began in 1958 with the banning of Tennessee Williams's play *Cat on a Hot Tin Roof*, on the grounds that it mentioned homosexuality.

The sheer absurdity of that decision might have been in keeping with the official morality of an establishment that still believed itself to be upholding the morals of some sexless Golden Age, but it flew in the face of even the most priggish interpretation of the country's laws. And, ten years later, something was done about it. From now on, public taste would be the primary arbiter of a play's suitability, and British theater exploded with new plays celebrating the ensuing freedom.

On September 27, 1968, twenty-four hours after the Theatres Act became law, the American hippie musical *Hair* opened at the Shaftsbury Theatre, the first show ever to openly present nudity, sexuality, blasphemy, and bad language on a London stage. And it proved, in case there was any doubt at all, that there was indeed a market in London for such things . . . a point that the last lingering critics declared was further belabored by the success two years later of Kenneth Tynan's *Oh! Calcutta!*

Opening in July 1970, *Oh! Calcutta!* was an oftentimes overly crude, but nevertheless essential purging of earlier moralities through a celebration of the utterly immoral.

Tynan referred to himself as the "thinking man's voyeur," and reveled in pre-opening night rumors that the play would be the first to feature live copulation on the off-Broadway stage (*Oh! Calcutta!* had opened in the United States a year earlier). At the same time, similar scuttlebutt revolved around the much-delayed release of Mick Jagger's first movie, *Performance.*

In fact, *Oh! Calcutta!* didn't live up to any of these promises, but audiences didn't care. To older theatergoers, it was the epitome of the new permissive society; to younger ones, it was a taste of a reality that they'd maybe only read about; and to the artistic ones, it was a challenge that would soon be met.

London, sadly, never received David Newburge's *Stag Movie*, a five-month off-Broadway wonder that starred the young Adrienne Barbeau and allegedly featured some of the finest sexual lyricism ever offered to the theater world (no cast album was ever recorded). But May 1971 brought the next American sensation to London, and this one really steamed. The London production of Tom Eyen and Jeff Barry's *The Dirtiest Show in Town* was produced (as were *Hair* and *Oh! Calcutta!*) by rock impresario Robert Stigwood and Michael White, one of British theater's most experienced and open-minded producers; it was controversial not only for its depictions of sex and flesh but also for its acknowledgment that gender should be no barrier to pleasure. "My play has no sex preference," Eyen said. "It's homo, hetero and bisexual. I'm not sticking up for any of the three."

Destined to run for almost 800 performances, *The Dirtiest Show in Town* took the West End by storm. More so than either of its naked predecessors, *The Dirtiest Show in Town* worked in the realm of actual political comment, as opposed to mere sound-byte rhetoric; it had a plot (of sorts) and purpose. More than that, however, it opened the door through which *The Rocky Horror Show*—another Michael White production, lest the linkage need further reinforcement—would sashay two years later, to become the first genuinely British theatrical production to both acknowledge the new themes running through the theatrical mainstream and employ them for something more than mere commentary.

Rocky Horror broached sexuality in guises that polite society still regarded, and maybe continues to regard, as deviant or dangerous, in a manner that at least requested understanding and examination; and again, the fact that it did so in tandem with the prevalent musical tastes of the day (most notably David Bowie's vision of a gay space invader) struck a blow against the still Victorian attitudes with which "polite society" viewed sexuality, in a manner that allowed an entire generation to begin openly questioning those attitudes.

Certainly that is the fate of Brad and Janet, the witless innocents who stumble so guilelessly out of a world of unremitting cleanliness and normalcy and into Frank-N-Furter's mansion of iniquity; and it is not even allegory to see them as personifying every teenager (and beyond) who was startled into acknowledging their own sexual needs by their simultaneous exposure to the glam rock tease. Bowie, by portraying himself as the first openly gay rock star, opened the door. But it was *The Rocky Horror Show* that held it open and suggested an entire generation pour through the crack.

Yet to view *The Rocky Horror Show* as simply a sexual liberator is to completely overlook its other attributes.

The early to mid 1970s was a time of intense nostalgia for the recent past. The Vietnam War continued to dominate the headlines, even in those countries (like Britain) that were completely uninvolved; in Britain itself, the last of a crippled right-wing Conservative government was crumbling in a sea of social disorder.

Unemployment was soaring so fast that only inflation could keep up with it, while those industries that were still working were riven by unrest and strikes. Entrance into the European Common Market (now the EEC) sent prices and taxes soaring even higher. And the country was reeling beneath a bombing campaign orchestrated by the Irish Republican Army, a series of explosions aimed at the highest profile targets the terrorists could infiltrate . . . or say they'd infiltrated, because they swiftly learned that just the suggestion of a planned bombing, a hoax phone call to the authorities or a newspaper, could bring great swathes of city life to a standstill. And not even *The Rocky Horror Show* was spared those attentions.

Against a backdrop as dark and foreboding as this, it was no surprise whatsoever that people in general, and artists in particular, were happier looking backward in time than forward to a future that could (and, pessimists delight, *would*) only get worse and worse. And the halcyon era, all seemed to agree, was the 1950s, those years when, with World War II won and a new affluence looming; with rock 'n' roll booming and Hollywood swinging; with science moving mountains and technology leaping over them, *anything* seemed possible.

In the United States, the stage show *Grease* and the movie *American Graffiti* both tapped into this passion for the past; in the UK, bands like Wizzard and Showaddywaddy re-created the sounds of the fifties on vinyl, while the movie *That'll Be the Day*, starring former *Godspell* front man David Essex, revisited them onscreen.

The Rocky Horror Show gnawed upon those emotions too. From the first words of the opening "Science Fiction/Double Feature" evocation of actor Michael Rennie, star of the classic sci-fi flick *The Day the Earth Stood Still*, *The Rocky Horror*

Show jerked every cinematic and pop cultural chain it could link to its plot, flashcard after flashcard of half-remembered imagery and incident that may have been paced as a stage show, but could have fit any artistic forum it chose . . . one reason the soundtrack exists not only as a souvenir of the stage show and the movie but even as an apparently open-mike recording of the audience's interaction with the film.

It is as a treasure trove of B movie nostalgia that *The Rocky Horror Show* perhaps makes its most dramatic point. And it did so close to a decade before sundry cinema historians began to reexamine Hollywood's cultist past, initially via Harry and Michael Medved's semisatirical *Golden Turkey Awards* digest of the world's "worst" movies (which, ironically, was responsible for introducing many people to its victims in the first place); and then on through a less condemnatory rediscovery of the so-called creature features.

Beginning again in the immediate postwar era, an incredible number of movies were made that posited sundry end-of-the-world scenarios. Often regarded as allegories of the Cold War paranoia that then gripped the United States and reached its political peak with McCarthy's communist witch hunt, movies such as *The Day the Earth Stood Still*, *Plan 9 from Outer Space*, *Attack of the Giant Leeches,* and so forth all examined the multitudinous ways mankind could be eliminated, with the increasingly bizarre nature of the killer creatures—some from outer space, others the result of man's own nuclear carelessness—seemingly rising and falling, depending upon just how evil the Soviet Union was *this* week.

Unlike so many conventional forms of propaganda, however, and in much the same way as *The Rocky Horror Show* has succeeded in transcending both its original content and context, the movies were also geared to entertain their audiences. Sophisticated modern viewers may now delight in looking back at the special effects that hallmarked these movies and complaining that they really aren't that special at all. At the time, however, nobody was looking for the feet beneath the piece of shag carpet that advances across the terrain (*The Creeping Terror*) or remarking upon the falling masonry that bounces like pieces of lightweight polystyrene (*Quatermass and the Pit*—a late-fifties TV series that was added to the cinematic canon in 1967). They simply thrilled to the chills of a small town encircled by—giant ants, killer crystals, radioactive mud, man-eating rabbits (somewhere, someone is still nursing a script in which bug-eyed bananas descend on the Midwest to wreak deadly havoc on all in their path), and anything else that the screenwriter could devise.

This same all-prevailing sense of innocence amid the allegory characterized *The Rocky Horror Show*; that, and the knowledge that, even as the cast waited backstage for the opening performance and actress Patricia Quinn prepared to raise the curtain with the first lines of the first song of the evening, the sixty-three expectant faces out in the audience were attending more than the first night of a new play.

They were witness to the first night of almost the entire cast's careers.

CHAPTER 2

How the Message Ran

The Rocky Horror Show was the brainchild of an actor who was essentially forced out of the London production of *Jesus Christ Superstar* when he suggested that King Herod (for whom he was understudy) be played as Elvis Presley. The producers, whose hands were on both the tiller and the purse strings, preferred him to tap dance. Neither party would budge, and Richard O'Brien quit the religious rock biz on the spot.

He filled his suddenly vacant time by writing a rock 'n' roll musical that would allow Elvis full rein, penning songs around a plotline lifted straight from the 1950s B movies that he loved so much. Born in Cheltenham, England, in 1942, O'Brien was a teen throughout that era, growing up with the infant yowlings of the newborn rock 'n' roll and the Cold War paranoia of period Hollywood schlock.

But he was also separated from those influences, not only by the customary dislocation that exists between audience and artist but also by distance. In 1952, when O'Brien was ten, his family relocated to a farm in Taraunga, New Zealand—the other side of the world in terms of geography; the other side of the universe in the realm of culture.

"New Zealand reminds me very much of the American mid-west," an older O'Brien told journalist Patricia Morrisroe. "There were two movie houses where I grew up. One showed all the latest releases and the other showed all the B-movies. I went to the movies a lot. What else can you do in a small-town parochial society? You see films, you play sports. If you were a bit of a punk like me you hung out in street corners and tried to pick up girls, not very successfully. The girls wanted to flirt but didn't want to be picked up. This was the fifties, remember."

He remained in New Zealand for the next decade but in 1962 returned to England, where he found work in careers as far apart as truck driving and hairdressing. He was also a keen horseman, a legacy of his days on the farm, and when he learned how valued that skill could be in show business, he put himself forward as a stuntman. Sharp-eyed observers may or may not spot O'Brien taking a tumble in such films as James Bond's *Casino Royale* and the comedy *Carry on Cowboy*; but such high-profile engagements only made him hanker for a life on the business end of the camera lens.

Working in whatever roles he could land, by 1969 O'Brien was appearing alongside another young actor, Tim Curry, in the touring production of *Hair* (he also met his first wife, Kimi Wong, in that show); his was a tiny role, however, and three years later, he was still struggling along, this time in the chorus of *Jesus Christ Superstar*. It was there that he hatched the notion of the infanticidal Herod being played as a biblical Elvis, and when his idea was dismissed, he resigned from the production.

Only one member of the *Jesus Christ Superstar* team appeared to sympathize with O'Brien: the production's Australian director, Jim Sharman.

James David Sharman was born in Sydney, Australia, on March 12, 1945. His father and grandfather ran a traveling sideshow, Jimmy Sharman's Boxing Troupe, and Sharman's formative years were spent in the twinned worlds of circus and traveling vaudeville. He went on to study production at the National Institute of Dramatic Art in Sydney.

"Though it may seem a big step from sideshows and circuses to mainstream theater, the distance is not so great," Sharman revealed in a lecture in 1995. "You have only to look below the surface of a seminal play like Samuel Beckett's

Waiting for Godot to sense a vaudeville routine waiting in the wings. The source of most sophisticated theater is to be found in popular culture. Directing Strindberg's *Dance of Death*, I was often reminded of Punch and Judy. Handke's *The Hour We Knew Nothing of Each Other* seems to owe something to that sight gag with a waiter constantly crossing the stage balancing an awkward tray. Gloria Dawn, the soubrette in Sorlie's *Varieties*, went on to play Mother Courage in an MTC production staged by a Berliner Ensemble director, and also played Mrs. Peachum in my staging of *The Threepenny Opera*. This production—in the opening season of the Drama Theatre of the Opera House—made a direct connection to the vaudeville tradition." Of course, *Rocky Horror* would allow these connections even greater rein.

After graduating in 1966, Sharman first came to wider attention with a series of experimental theater productions at the Old Tote in Sydney, but it was his production of Mozart's *Don Giovanni* for Opera Australia that truly confirmed his reputation. At the Old Tote, incidentally, Sharman first worked alongside Brian Thomson, the set designer with whom he has been associated for much of his subsequent career.

Over the next six years, Sharman was involved in two of the era's most revolutionary plays, as producer of the Australian productions of *Hair* (which also took him to Tokyo and

Boston) and *Jesus Christ Superstar*. The latter brought him to the attention of the play's lyricist, Tim Rice, and by 1972 Sharman was in the UK, handling the London version of the same stage show. He also oversaw a production of American playwright Sam Shepard's *The Unseen Hand*. Having taken a liking to O'Brien during his brief span at *Superstar*, Sharman quickly handed him his next major acting role, the part of Willie the Space Freak.

In the meantime, O'Brien had discovered another role to play—that of aspiring songsmith. He was constantly writing during this period, not only amassing a plethora of songs but also forming a conceptual framework in his mind that encompassed not only his musical tastes but also his cinematic fantasies. The first pages of what would become *Rocky Horror* were born there.

"I never wanted to be a writer," O'Brien once said. "Acting was always the important thing in my life. I had no desire to be an *actor*, and do Shakespeare. I didn't want to be a celebrity. I just wanted to play make-believe. It was all very child-like. Very simple." He wrote to kill time; it was, he said, "a way for me to spend winter evenings when I was an out of work actor. It was the very first thing I'd ever written. I didn't even see it as writing, really. I was just having a ball."

A conversation with Jim Sharman gave the ball its bounce. O'Brien later admitted, "Writing *Rocky* was almost like working on a jigsaw puzzle. I had written several of the songs before and all I had to do was slot them in. I didn't start at the beginning and develop the plot from there. I started at both ends and then filled in the middle." But it was not until he showed it to Sharman, sang him some of the songs, let the Australian's experience guide his own enthusiasm, and then unleashed the vision that their shared creativity brought to the surface that O'Brien conceded that he'd actually written a stage show. Before, it was still just a piece of fun.

He did not remain in the dark for long. With his long-running sidekick Brian Thomson naturally confirmed as set designer, Sharman began recruiting both cast and crew.

He started at the top, with producer Michael White—the coproducer behind *The Dirtiest Show in Town*, but also a guiding force behind many of the other crucial productions of the previous decade: *The Connection* in 1961, *Saturday Night and Sunday Morning* in 1966, *Sleuth* in 1969. He came close to being the first to present Andy Warhol's seminal Velvet Underground in the UK in 1967, stymied only by time constraints and the demands of his work with Joe Orton's *Loot*; and, of course, he teamed with Robert Stigwood for *Hair*, *Oh! Calcutta!*, and *The Dirtiest Show in Town*. In confronting the British theatergoing public with the unusual, risqué, and controversial, White had no peer.

Neither, as it transpired, did the man selected to take the leading role in the play. Born in Grappenhall, England, on April 19, 1946, Timothy James Curry—the actor entrusted with that particular majestic part—was the son of a Royal Navy Methodist chaplain, James, and a school secretary, Patricia. A boy soprano in his local church at six and a Shakespearean actor at ten (albeit in a school production), Curry attended boarding school in Bath, then studied drama and English at Birmingham University. He graduated with a combined degree, and his roommate, fellow drama student Patrick Barlow, recalled the moment he first realized that Curry was going to be a success.

They were seated high up in London's Palace Theatre, watching actress Judi Dench appear as Sally Bowles in the original run of Christopher Isherwood's *Cabaret*. Dench had the stage to herself, a single figure in a spotlight, holding the entire audience spellbound in her palm. Suddenly Curry whispered to Barlow, "*That's* what I want to be." Days—just twenty-four hours, in fact—later, he and Barlow tried out for a street theater troupe in Chalk Farm, and Curry landed his first major role, in *Hair*.

He remained with that production until early 1970, following up with further study and engagements as far apart (geographically speaking) as the Royal Court in London and the Glasgow Civic Repertory Company. At the time of his casting as Frank-N-Furter, however, he remained unknown to the public at large . . . an unknown, continued Barlow, with an amazing voice. "It was just completely perfect, just something he was born with—it came ready made. We would go to university parties and end up having a drink and whatever and he would break out into song, this marvelous bluesy voice."

Sharman recalls his first ever glimpse of Curry at the audition. "There may have been other actors that I considered initially for the role of Frank. I can't remember them. I just remember Tim Curry walked through the door of the Royal Court Theatre saying 'rip it up.' And he got the role."

Curry also would prove to be a natural to the costume he was to wear for the production. Two years earlier, working alongside a brilliant young costume designer named Sue Blane on Lindsay Kemp's production of Jean Genet's *The Maids*, Curry had been cast in the role of Solange, and sent onstage every night in a tight black corset. When Blane too was recruited for this new production, one of her first acts was to contact Kemp and ask for that same corset back. Blane's original vision of Frank-N-Furter as a platinum blonde was quickly dispensed with (along with the German accent that Curry was toying with—he replaced it with what he described as a combination of the Queen and his mother's telephone voice), but the corset remained. And so did one other lingering impression, best conveyed by Roger Baker, author of the definitive guide to female impersonation in the performing arts, *Drag*.

> Perhaps [Greta] Garbo's greatest screen role, Queen Christina [was] a seventeenth century Swedish monarch with a penchant for wearing male attire and almost certainly a lesbian . . . [allowing] the star to fully exploit her ambiguity. Interestingly, Garbo's appearance in this film is echoed by . . . Curry . . . [who] made bodices, stockings and suspenders almost *de rigueur* among heterosexual men.

The finishing touch, however, was the largest available women's shoes, into which Curry was just able to squeeze his size eights. "The shoes were very important," Curry said at the time. "I didn't get near the part until very late in rehearsal, and I said 'I must have the shoes.' Then it all happened. I tend to work from the feet upwards."

Designer Blane was not initially keen on *Rocky Horror*. "I thought the story sounded awful. I had no desire to design a lot of drag costumes for no money. I had enough work at the time not to have to take on something unless it paid a lot or it was great fun. And from what I imagined, *Rocky* didn't promise to be fun at all."

A meeting with Jim Sharman changed her mind. "Jim and I got along like a house on fire. While he was outlining the plot we got incredibly drunk and then went around to the Royal Court Theatre. When I realized that Tim Curry and some other friends of mine were going to be in it, I thought, 'Oh, this is beginning to sound like a wonderful idea.' By three o'clock in the morning, with the start of a terrible hangover, I was doing *Rocky*."

Armed with a $400 budget, she began touring London's thrift stores and flea markets, collecting the props she knew would be invaluable, fashioning the costumes from pieces discovered in junk shops and flea markets around London. "With such a small budget, everything *had* to be junk. There was no way around it."

"The casting of Frank-N-Furter [was] crucial," O'Brien told *The Scotsman* newspaper. "Wit and intelligence is what you need. And that sense of danger, that he might climb over the footlights and roger the wife—and he may well roger the husband as well. It's that kind of ambivalence that makes him dangerous and appealing, cheeky and charming, charismatic and selfish and all the things that he is."

Curry himself has frequently played down the significance of the role, particularly in relation to his own career—he is, after all, one of Britain's busiest and best-loved film and theater performers. In a particularly ill-tempered interview in 1979, at the height of what ultimately became a short-lived career as a rock 'n' roll performer, an exasperated Curry finally snapped after receiving one *Rocky Horror* question too many.

"It was a play. I was doing this one particular role in London for about a year, and *Rocky Horror* was the next one that came up for the theater I was in. They asked me to do the title role. I was performing in a 60-seat experimental playhouse called the Royal Court Theatre. This particular building held two theaters—one held about 800 people, the other 60. They were always looking for writers, and this play came in the door.

"The play was a big success in London and then it moved to Los Angeles. It drew big crowds there as well. Then the powers that be decided to make it into a motion picture. They made the Broadway show into a movie and it turned out to be a flop. Twentieth Century didn't like the film very much, didn't put any promotion behind it, and just let it slip into midnight movie rotation on the weekends. Suddenly, the film started to work and it literally took on a life of its own from that point on. [But] I look at it as something I did in 1974. That's exactly how I look at the movie. It's a piece of work I did five years ago.

"Journalists come to my show with preconceived notions of who I am. They know they can get column space in their papers because of . . . *Rocky Horror.* . . . They can always say, 'Well, he wasn't as good as the movie.' They can write six inches of copy alongside of a guy wearing a corset and stockings then get into a heavy metaphysical speculation about the image. I never gave a shit about my image."

He would have been the only person who felt that way.

"The element of transvestism wasn't intended as a major theme, although it turned out to be one," Richard O'Brien admitted. "Writing a transvestite into the play was a very naive judgment. Maybe there was a lot of subconscious feeling about that subject coming through. I don't know. I've always thought of Frank as a cross between Ivan the Terrible and Cruella de Vil of Walt Disney's *One Hundred and One Dalmatians*. It's that sort of evil beauty that's attractive. I found Brad and Janet very appealing too, especially the whole fifties image of boy-girl relationships. In the end, you see that Janet is not the weak little thing that society demands her to be and Brad is not the pillar of strength."

At the same time, however, Curry's image could be taken too far. In 2010, O'Brien recalled, "There was one time I will never forget. It was the thirty year anniversary at the Queens theatre for three weeks and that first night I was in the downstairs bar of the theatre and there was a man climbing up the stairs, and I mean climbing up the stairs. He was on his hands and knees because the heels of his shoes were far too high to walk on—they were fetish shoes and you just couldn't walk on them. So he was climbing and his arms were splayed and his knees were ambling up and his arse was in the air and he has a leather thong on and a hairy arse and I remember thinking 'oh that is so disgusting, that is dreadful'. And then I thought [his head in hands], 'oh dear God, Oh God, I'm partially responsible for this. I've given this person the opportunity to do this.' I was so horrified and I was culpable."

With Curry the magisterial star of the show and O'Brien cast as the antihero Riff Raff, the search was on for further unconventional blood to pack the remainder of the cast.

For the role of Magenta, Frank-N-Furter's sex-on-wheels maid, there were hopes that singer Marianne Faithfull might be recruited. The notion was stillborn. An accomplished actress since making her debut in Chekhov's *Three Sisters* at the Royal Court in 1969, Faithfull was now at the height of her tabloid notoriety as the fallen angel of British pop, struggling to rebuild a career that had been ravaged by drugs and heartbreak. She would have been an inspired and perhaps even inspiring choice, but it was not to be.

Her "replacement" was nevertheless a masterstroke.

Born on May 28, 1944, Belfast native Patricia Quinn began her acting career as a member of the British Drama League in Belfast. She trained at the Drama Centre and by 1971 was appearing in repertory with the Glasgow Citizen's

Theatre. Like Tim Curry, she also appeared at the Royal Court, earning considerable acclaim for her role in Heathcote Williams's *AC/DC*.

She was also working for a time as a blackjack-dealing bunny at the London Playboy Club, but only until her acting career took off. By the time *The Rocky Horror Show* came around, she was just beginning to move into television too, with appearances in such fondly recalled British series as the comedy *The Fenn Street Gang*, the crime drama *Van der Valk*, and *Saturday Night Theatre*.

Quinn recalled her introduction to the world of *Rocky Horror*.

"I auditioned for the play and it was a singing audition and they wanted a sort of rock & roll song as the audition piece. I turned up singing a 1930's Jessie Matthews number. But that suited the part of the usherette singing 'Science Fiction.' Richard played 'Science Fiction' for me on the guitar, at the audition. And he said: 'Can you just sing along with this a bit.' I was very nervous, and I tried to. I thought they were rock & roll guys and I didn't know how to do all this."

Clearly she made the right impression, though. "Afterwards I went skipping down the road and I thought: 'This is fantastic.' It was one of the best songs I'd ever heard. I went home and told my agent I wanted to do it. And he said: 'You haven't read the script yet.' And I said, 'I know, but I still want to do it.' And he said, 'it might be a song and four lines,' [and when] I collected my script and turned page after page, [I] counted four lines. But I didn't care how big the part was; I wanted to sing that song. So that was it. I didn't read the whole script at all before I agreed to do it—I only read my own bit. Like most actors do. You can get into a lot of trouble doing that, actually."

The youngest of the play's principal characters (at least among those who moved on to the movie) was Laura Elizabeth Campbell, a Sydney, Australia–born actress whose twentieth birthday, May 24, fell just three weeks before *The Rocky Horror Show* opened.

Nicknamed "Little Nell" by her father, a popular Australian newspaper columnist, Campbell kept that name when her family moved to London in the early 1970s. For a time she ran a small but flourishing boutique in London's Kensington Market; quite coincidentally, her stall was next door to one run by the then-unknown Freddie Bursali . . . Freddie Mercury to be.

She also earned money as a busker on the London streets, and it was her tap dancing routines, learned as a child and honed on the pavements of the city, that assured her the role of Columbia in the play. Jim Sharman caught one of her performances one day and immediately brought her into the play—hastily informing Richard O'Brien that he needed to write in a new character and songs to accommodate her. The role of Columbia, a groupie who has attached herself to Frank-N-Furter, was not a part of the original script.

The other major characters in the original cast included Julie Covington as Janet Weiss (replaced by Belinda Sinclair, after Covington took a role in the Globe Theatre's presentation of *Antony and Cleopatra*), Christopher Malcolm as Brad Majors, Rayner Bourton as Rocky, Paddy O'Hagan in the twin roles of Eddie and Dr. Everett Scott, and Jonathan Adams as the Narrator. And Adams became the fifth member of the London cast to be invited to appear in the movie, although not as Narrator; rather, he was cast as Dr. Scott, after declaring himself bored with his original role.

Born in Northampton, England, on February 14, 1931, John "Jonathan" Adams had his own story to tell about the power of the creature feature—it was a childhood viewing of *The Cabinet of Dr. Caligari* that decided him to become an actor and an artist in the first place, parallel careers in which he would excel. It was the latter, art, that consumed Adams's attention through his teens and twenties; he did not seriously move into acting until the age of twenty-eight, in 1959, following two years' compulsory service in the Royal Air Force and four post-demobilization years as a school-teacher. He took the name Jonathan Adams, incidentally, because the actors' union Equity already had a John Adams on their books.

Still, his acting career very much played second fiddle to his continuing exploits in the art world; he seemed doomed to repertory, interspersed with spells as a substitute teacher, until *The Rocky Horror Show* came along, and although he continued to work thereafter, it remains his best remembered role. In fact, the only question Adams ever asked when he was reminded of the fact was, "Which role are you thinking of?" His Narrator and his Dr. Scott were equally memorable.

CHAPTER 3

"Science Fiction/Double Feature"

Richard O'Brien originally composed "Science Fiction/ Double Feature" as a stand-alone song, to be performed at a Christmas party at Elstree Studios in 1972. Yet it is also the song that gives shape to the entire Rocky Horror Show.

Patricia Quinn was the first person to sing the song on the Rocky Horror stage; when she returned to the production for the movie in 1974, she naturally assumed the song would remain hers. In fact, O'Brien himself voices it over the movie credits, and maybe that was the wrong decision. There are few moments so memorable on the 1973 original cast LP as the sound of Quinn pouring her all into a lyric that, quite simply, encapsulates great swathes of the movie's momentum.

As the darkened stage is split by a pair of giant red lips, lascivious and lewd, recounting the great sci-fi stars and movies of the past, from *The Invisible Man* to *The Day of the Triffids,* from Claude Rains to Janette Scott, thirty-plus years of creature features are name-checked and nuanced, setting a stage . . . but for what?

The Ultimate Creature Feature

A quick guide to the songs that are singled out for attention . . . a science fiction double feature indeed. Few movie themes have ever proved so self-fulfillingly prophetic as that which opens *The Rocky Horror Show*: "Science Fiction/Double Feature," looking back on the late-night double features that were once a staple of the cinema circuit (before television adapted the concept for itself) and would essentially be reborn as a vehicle for *The Rocky Horror Picture Show.*

THE DAY OF THE TRIFFIDS
Author John Wyndham's tale of mankind under attack from a race of malignant plant life was an established literary classic long before any attempt was made to translate it to film or TV—a process that continues into the twenty-first century. Arguably, none of the adaptations has been as successful as the original book, but the 1962 movie is the most charming, as American leading man Howard Keel (*Seven Brides for Seven Brothers, Dallas,* etc.) rounds up the likes of Nicole Maurey, Mervyn Johns, and Janette Scott to lead mankind's defense.

"Dammit, Janet!"

Certainly nothing that need concern the newly affianced Brad Majors and Janet Weiss, as they depart a friend's wedding (Janet caught the bouquet, of course) for a visit with their old tutor, Dr. Scott. Behind them, the wedding party fades from view, although one of the bridesmaids, actress

NIGHT OF THE DEMON
Released in the United States as *Curse of the Demon* (although one wonders what difference that one word made?), this 1957 occult thriller features Dana Andrews as the hero who, according to the song, was given the runes by prunes. A healthy pun, then, although no preparation for the satanic cavorting that makes this movie such a joy.

IT CAME FROM OUTER SPACE
From 1953, a pioneer of the 3D technology that has made such a comeback (or not) in recent years, *It Came from Outer Space* was also one of the first movies to suggest that maybe those bug-eyed, tentacle-waving monsters inside the flying saucer are as frightened of (and repulsed by) us as we are of them—and in any case, mean no harm. Would we still want to blast them into oblivion?

Of course we would. We must protect ourselves, after all.

KING KONG
The classic monkey movie, and there's no need to say any more. In answer to Frank-N-Furter wistfully demanding to know to know

Continues on next page

Koo Stark, would later shoot to British tabloid immortality as the (in some quarters) controversial girlfriend of Prince Andrew.

"Over at the Frankenstein Place"

Chatting as young lovers do, and moralizing on the stupid behavior of the phalanx of bikers that passes them on the

Continued

"whatever happened to Fay Wray," however . . . well, she also appeared in . . .

DOCTOR X

A 1932 "we know whodunnit," in which a party of eccentric doctors are invited to reenact the hideous crimes of one of their number, in the hope that the true killer might reveal himself. Lionel Atwill and Lee Tracy star alongside the elfin Ms. Wray, but it's the Full Moon Killer who wins the viewer's support.

THE DAY THE EARTH STOOD STILL

Another reminder that not everybody who knocks on your front door is going to be a masked marauder. Sometimes it's just the mailman, delivering a box of goodwill and cheer from the friendly neighbors on the other side of the galaxy. Two years before *It Came from Outer Space* came from outer space, *The Day the Earth Stood Still* starred Michael Rennie as the ambassadorial Klaatu; Lock Martin as Gort, a winding, rainswept road, Brad and Janet do not have a care in the world. But on this archetypically dark and stormy night, a sudden flat tire quickly catches them off guard.

Abandoning the car while they go in search of a phone, the pair spot and follow a light burning on the top floor of a nearby castle. They enter the grounds to find that this was also the destination for the constant stream of motorcycles

seven-foot-tall robot; and Patricia Neal as the Earth girl who befriends them both.

FORBIDDEN PLANET
We are less than a century now from the year in which this gem was set, a 1956 space epic in which a landing on the planet Altair IV is disrupted and almost destroyed by an invisible entity that can only be seen when it touches the spaceship's force field. Leslie Nielsen, Warren Stevens, and Earl Holliman are the travelers sent to rescue the pioneering Dr. Morbius (Walter Pidgeon) and his daughter, Alta (Anne Francis), but all pale alongside the movie's most memorable icon, Robby the Robot.

THE INVISIBLE MAN
Claude Rains became a superstar after appearing (or not) in the title role of this 1933 movie, an adaptation of the H. G. Wells classic story. Arguably part of the same wave of moral moviemaking that created *Reefer Madness* and sundry other antidrug flicks of the era, *The Invisible Man* set the scene for a host of other films that are bent on reminding us that, even when

Continues on next page

they'd noticed earlier in the evening. But they do not see the strange, crooked figure who watches their arrival; nor do they expect the humpbacked vision, Riff Raff, who opens the front door with one of the most unforgettable greetings in cinematic history: "You're wet."

"The Time Warp"

"The master," explains the peculiar doorman, is hosting one of his functions—an annual Transylvanian Convention,

---

Continued

science tries to do us all a favor (nuclear power is our friend, remember, and monocaine could have been useful for something), it still has a capacity for inadvertently doing wrong. A theme that is revisited in . . .

TARANTULA
Leo G. Carroll is the scientist who inadvertently transforms a regular arachnoid into a frenzied eight-legged killing machine; the young Clint Eastwood is among the fighter pilots sent out to destroy it.

WHEN WORLDS COLLIDE
The colliding world is, in fact, a falling star, passing close enough to the Earth to set off a chain reaction of cataclysmic disasters. The only hope is to load as many of Earth's population onto a space ship as possible . . . which, typically, is basically no more than a handful of smart ones. The rest of us are left to perish (nice), while the eggheads rebuild humanity on the planet Zyra.

into which the wet and trembling Brad and Janet are ushered.

There is a wonderful and often overlooked echo here of a movie that followed a similar tack just four years earlier—Nicolas Roeg's Performance, starring the Frank-that-never-was, Mick Jagger, also charts the progress (and decline) of an "innocent abroad" in a sea of countercultural chaos, an on-the-run gangster who rents a room in the gothicly furnished home of a reclusive junkie pop star. The scene where gangster Chas is reduced to all but pleading for the use of Jagger's phone is deliciously reflected in Brad and Janet's own, constantly rebuffed attempts to use the castle's.

And while Chas is drawn into an increasingly claustrophobic world of drugs and sex, with the undercurrent of violence eddying around every nuance, Brad and Janet find no claustrophobia, no undercurrents, and, for the moment, not yet any Eddie. Instead, they are invited to meet the Transylvanians, party guests who are the movie's greatest departure from the stage show: outlandishly clad, ostentatiously mannered, they are clearly intended to provide the still unseen master with the sycophantic audience that he demands. Included among their ranks, incidentally, were O'Brien's wife, Kimi Wong, and a young Christopher Biggins, later to establish himself as one of Britain's best-loved character actors. But who has the time to notice that? Instead we are incited to watch as revelers and servants alike dance "The Time Warp."

The best-known song in the movie, incidentally, also came close to not even being a part of it. "The Time Warp" was composed and included only after Little Nell revealed her tap-dancing prowess, and Jim Sharman requested a song that would allow her to demonstrate it.

"Sweet Transvestite"

Backed into a corner, Brad and Janet turn as an elevator begins its rattling approach, its descent only slowly revealing the outlandish appearance of its occupant, the leonine Frank-N-Furter. Around them cavort the master's minions—Riff Raff, the handyman; Magenta, his sister; and Columbia, the groupie.

"The Sword of Damocles" and "I Can Make You a Man"

Resplendent in a backless green surgical gown, Frank explains that he has discovered the "secret to life itself," and proceeds to demonstrate his discovery by indeed bringing to life a shapeless bundle of bandages submerged in a tank of water. Before the assembled gaze of his astonished party guests, he relives every great Frankenstein movie of the past by jolting life into . . . Rocky. Who promptly jolts his creator by fleeing from his none-too-subtle sexual advances.

"I Can Make You a Man" (and its reprise, later in the performance) was the first of two songs excluded from the original seventy-minute stage presentation; "Sword of Damocles," meanwhile, was absent from original vinyl pressings of the soundtrack LP.

"Hot Patootie—Bless My Soul"

In classic Frankenstein style, Frank created Rocky from elements of a host of other bodies. Unlike his predecessor, he was not so careful about disposing of them. Eddie, a rock 'n' rolling delivery boy and a former lover of Columbia, was the unwilling donor of a part of Rocky's brain and has spent his postoperative period in a large freezer—from which he now emerges, only to be slaughtered again, in full view of the assembled hordes, by an ice axe-wielding Frank.

"I Can Make You a Man—Reprise"

Furter and Rocky retire to the bridal suite, but Rocky flees again, returning to his tank, where he is discovered by Riff Raff and Magenta. They begin to torment him, while Frank goes in search of other conquests.

"Touch-a, Touch-a, Touch-a, Touch Me"

The final song to be added to the script, just days before the first preview.

Shown to separate bedrooms for the night, Brad and Janet also retire. Janet's rest, however, is soon disturbed by the arrival of a man she thinks is Brad—only to discover, once they are in bed together, that it is Frank in disguise. Confused by the sudden, unexpected loss of her treasured virginity, Janet is further shattered when, leaving her room to find Brad, she instead discovers a video monitor playing the scene now taking place in her fiance's bedroom, as he too is seduced by Frank.

She flees, only to discover Rocky still cowering in his tank, nursing the wounds inflicted upon him by Riff Raff and Magenta. She bandages him and then gently begins to seduce him. In their own room, Magenta and Columbia watch and laugh.

"Eddie's Teddy"

This is the second of two songs excluded from the original theatrical presentation of The Rocky Horror Show.

Searching for the missing Rocky and Janet, Frank, Brad, and Riff Raff now discover that an intruder has entered the building—Dr. Everett Scott, Brad and Janet's old high school science teacher and, it transpires, the late Eddie's uncle. Frank also knows Scott, and believes him to be a government

TOP: A button commemorating the first anniversary of *Rocky* opening at the Plaza Twin in February 1981.

BOTTOM: Something for the Transylvanian with everything—the *Rocky* "complete" make-up kit.

LEFT: The original movie soundtrack album.

RIGHT: An original movie flyer.

TOP: A handout from the Varsity Theatre in University City, Missouri.

BOTTOM LEFT: With a nightly lineup like this, it's no wonder the city never sleeps. New York's 8th Street Playhouse lines *Rocky* up with Mick Jagger's *Performance*, Andy Warhol's *Bad*, and a Pasolini trilogy.

BOTTOM RIGHT: The original Australian theatrical cast album.

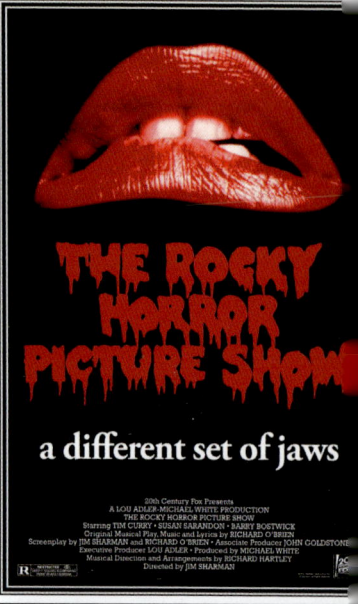

TOP LEFT: The *Rocky* DVD.

TOP RIGHT: One of producer Lou Adler's most memorable period quotes lives on into the DVD age.

BOTTOM: A *Rocky*-themed AIDS fundraiser from London, Ontario, in 2010.

TOP: It was great when it all began, and it's still great today. Pages from the Broadway revival program.

LEFT: Brad Armstrong's brilliant *Rocky* porn parody.

TOP: A charity screening of *Rocky* in Portsmouth, England.

LEFT: *Rocky* celebrates Halloween in Nashville, October 2010.

TOP: Another city, another *Rocky*!

RIGHT: Bellevue Community College, Washington, produced *Rocky* in 2007.

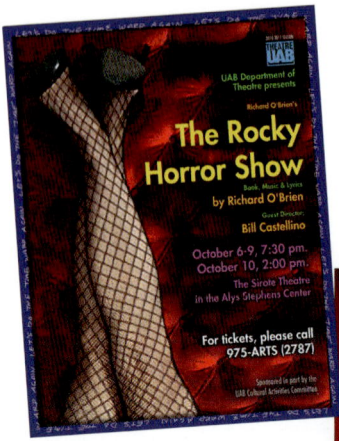

TOP: *Rocky* visits Birmingham, Alabama.

RIGHT: They said it couldn't last. New York's Beacon Theater marks ten years of midnight showings.

agent investigating UFOs. Upon discovering that Brad and Janet are friends of the doctor, he begins to suspect a plot.

First, however, a meal. A sumptuous spread is served, and only once it is under way and Scott is recalling his missing nephew does Frank reveal the true nature of the food. It was Eddie.

"Wise up, Janet Weiss" (a.k.a. "Planet Schmanet Janet")

Another song excised from the original soundtrack LP accompanies Janet as she flees the dining room with Rocky, while Frank prepares his revenge on all of his guests: a Medusa Transducer that transforms them into living statues.

"Rose Tint My World": The Floor Show— "Fanfare/Don't Dream It"—"Wild and Untamed Thing"

While the statues perform a live cabaret floor show, orchestrated by a Judy Garland-esque Frank, Riff Raff and Magenta emerge in full space-age regalia, demanding that they return to their home planet, Transsexual, in the galaxy of Transylvania.

"I'm Going Home"

O'Brien originally wrote the movie's climactic ballad for his wife to sing as part of their own Kimi and Ritz act; it is one of several songs composed with other ends in mind, and then shoehorned into the Rocky Horror concept (incredibly, "Over at the Frankenstein Place" is another).

Frank reluctantly agrees to his minions' demand, believing that he too will return to sweet Transsexual. Magenta and Riff Raff have other plans, however; they kill Columbia, Rocky, and Frank and release Brad, Janet, and Dr. Scott. Then the entire castle blasts off into space.

"Science Fiction/Double Feature—Reprise"

The closing credits roll.

The Singers, Not the Songs

A multitude of *Rocky Horror* cast recordings notwithstanding, no fewer than four of the movie's eight principal actors have enjoyed recording careers alongside—and maybe even as an adjunct to—their success in the movie.

The most prominent of these, of course, is Meat Loaf—author of one of the best-selling albums of all time, 1977's *Bat Out of Hell*. His thirty-plus-year career since then has established him as one of rock's most respected and versatile performers, regardless of the occasional ebb and flow of his commercial popularity.

He was also, courtesy of the *Stoney and MeatLoaf* LP, the first of the recognized cast members (stage or screen) to record a long-playing record, two years before the movie opened.

Little Nell too had some early recording experience, after she was recruited as a guest vocalist on the single "Tuff Little Surfer Boy" by Truth & Beauty in 1974; and 1975 saw Richard O'Brien and wife Kim united as the singing duo Kimi and Ritz. That year they released two singles in the UK: the seasonal "Merry Christmas Baby"/"Eddie" ("Eddie's Teddy," from the *Rocky Horror Show*) and "I Was in Love with Danny, But the Crowd Was in Love with Dean"/"Pseuds Corner" (titled for a popular feature in the satirical magazine *Private Eye*). Neither sold especially well, although the Christmas single did brisk business after it was added to the merchandise stall at the King's Road Theatre.

In the event, and hardly surprisingly, Tim Curry's recording career was the first out of the starter's gate in the wake of *The Rocky Horror Picture Show*, when he went into the studio to cut a full album for movie producer Lou Adler's Ode label.

It was an eclectic bag; the nine-song set initially threatened to pick up where the movie soundtrack left off, with Curry's vocals stepping straight out of Frank-N-Furter's diction and demeanor before lapsing into a more generic mid-1970s soft-rock vein.

Nevertheless, its best moments continued to dance on the edge of innuendo and smut, against a musical accompaniment that toys with reggae, R&B, rock, and even an oddly effective, slowed-down pout through the Supremes' "Baby Love." Like the man himself, it was a ferociously individual collection of songs; unlike the man, it was doomed to obscurity.

It would be another thirty-four years before the sessions were released, as the aptly titled *From the Vaults* CD. The album's original disappearance was rendered all the more surprising by the release, in 1976, of another LP from the *Rocky Horror* family, Little Nell's *The Musical*

Continues on next page

Continued

World of Little Nell—Aquatic Teenage Sex & Squalor, and a savage slice of controversy when she appeared on British television to perform her debut single, "Do the Swim"—and accidentally exposed her breasts to the watching audience . . . several times.

Three further Little Nell singles—"Fever" in 1978, "Beauty Queen" in 1979, and "Tropical Isle" in 1980—followed, but the focus switched back to Tim Curry with the release, also in 1978, of *Read My Lips,* a predominantly covers-heavy set that included a storming version of the Move's "Brontosaurus," a reggaefied take on the Beatles' "I Will," and a bagpipe-laden romp through "Wake Nicodemus."

Recorded with a superstar roster of accompanying musicians, including Nils Lofgren, former Lou Reed/Alice Cooper sideman Dick Wagner, renowned New York keyboard player Michael Kamen, and producer Bob Ezrin, *Read My Lips* was not a hit. But friendly reviews and a burgeoning cult following prompted Curry to cut a follow-up, the self-professedly "thump and bump"-ing *Fearless,* and this time, there was a response. Two minor American hit singles spun off the LP, "I Do the Rock" and "Paradise Garage," whose accompanying video included an appearance by Dori Hartley, one of the ringleaders of *Rocky Horror*'s Waverly Theater success.

Curry also toured the United States in support of the record, putting on an energetic show that highlighted the best of both LPs (but firmly omitted any reference to *Rocky Horror*), and a string of often confrontational interviews saw him taking the role of a rock star very seriously indeed.

It was not to be, however. A third LP, *Simplicity,* was released in 1981 and went nowhere; highlights of all three solo albums would later be combined on *The Best of Tim Curry.*

The musical was still known as *They Came from Denton High* (and the character of Brad was still named Ricky) when, shortly before the first of two scheduled preview performances, Sharman suggested it be retitled *The Rocky Horror Show*.

The 70-minute play then opened on schedule at the Royal Court's 63-seat Theatre Upstairs, a project space set aside for new and experimental work, on June 19, 1973, with two performances (9 P.M., 11 P.M.) nightly until July 20. There *The Rocky Horror Show* found its legs.

Downstairs at the main theater, Vincent Price and Coral Browne were appearing in a production of Edward Bond's *The Sea*; following their performance, they ventured up to the tiny Upstairs room to watch *Rocky Horror*. Both fell in love with it—and so did everybody else, even those, like *Daily Mail* theater critic Jack Tinker, who spent their lives watching theater. His review didn't even mention that it was a musical; he simply called it the most brilliant piece of theater he'd seen in a long time.

Producer Michael White too was astonished by the success of the evening. O'Brien recalled "Michael White coming up to me after the first night and saying, 'I think we've got a hit, Richard.' I said, 'Oh, that's nice,' and walked away. It just didn't register." More than thirty years later, he told the British *Independent* newspaper that the play's success was the biggest shock of his life. "The original run was three weeks. I was expecting to be looking for another job. It really was a crowd-pleaser and people are still interacting with it [today]."

By the end of its second night, *The Rocky Horror Show* had been signed up for a full cast album, after English record producer and habitual hit maker Jonathan King—lured into earshot by the *Daily Mail* review—caught the show and grabbed the rights on the spot. With Belinda Sinclair filling in for Julie Covington, the album would be recorded in August, during one manic twenty-four-hour session at SARM East Studios in London.

King would also become heavily involved in the show's initial promotion, while throwing his own financial weight behind the production, joining Michael White as its principal backer. His UK Records label was still a fledgling at the time, just a handful of singles old. But the *Rocky Horror Show* original cast recording, along with the band 10cc and King himself, would place UK firmly on the British musical map.

With the end of the play's original run in sight, demand for seats every night wasn't simply outstripping supply, it was even testing London's traditionally so resourceful black market. The Royal Court extended the play's initial three-week run to five; by August, Michael White was suggesting that the play be transferred to the West End, the established home of London theater.

O'Brien refused. *Rocky Horror* demanded intimacy and, in a way, obscurity; it was a little jewel to be discovered glistening off the beaten track of the theatrical establishment. Plus, it was written and designed with a very specific type of venue in mind, one that could, in essence, be imagined as a movie theater. Which is when, with perfect synchronicity, the production was offered space at the larger Classic Cinema, farther along the King's Road in *über*-fashionable Chelsea.

It was an approach that stepped straight back to Sharman's own vaudevillian upbringing, as he acknowledged during a 1995 lecture at the Belvoir Street Theatre in Sydney, Australia. "Brian Thomson's blue-canvased cinema-under-demolition set turned virtually every theater or old cinema we played in into a tent. The transvestite hero of that musical might have owed something to German gothic cinema, but was also derived from childhood memories of Bobby Le Brun, Sorlie's famous Panto Dame, who looked like a stevedore in drag. Tim Curry, who created Frank in my original production at the Royal Court, kept asking, 'How far should I go?' and I always replied, 'Just stop before you throw Fantales to the kiddies.' The audience thought they were seeing a hip, streetwise character in a rock 'n' roll show; we knew it was a panto dame in mufti."

The play's final night at the Royal Court, however, was not the triumph it could have been—it was canceled after

Rayner Bourton, the titular Rocky, managed to get some glitter down the front of his silver briefs—in the days when glitter was made from tiny pieces of glass—and needed to visit the hospital for treatment. Among the sixty-three ticket holders left disappointed in the stalls were Mick and Bianca Jagger, playwright Pam Gems, and actor Elliott Gould.

Patricia Quinn was staggered by the play's success. "I could never imagine that at the time, except when we first started doing it on the stage. I would go backstage to this little office to change from the usherette to Magenta, and if people turned up late they would have to come in through this office. I was there one day and (Rudolf) Nureyev came through. Later we had Vincent Price and Mick Jagger, all coming to see this musical in a 60-seat theatre."

Reopening at the Classic, *Rocky* was billed on the street with a poster that sought to remind passersby that it *was* a play, not what the London magazine *Time Out* described as "one of the B-Movies it so successfully sends up": *The Rocky Horror Show Alive on Stage*. With two new songs added to the running order, "The Charles Atlas Song" (later retitled "I Can Make You a Man") and its reprise and "Eddie's Teddy," the schedule shifted to a more traditional eight performances per week, with two shows every Friday and Saturday, but none on Sundays.

The Classic was only ever a temporary home; the 270-seat building was scheduled for demolition. *The Rocky Horror Show* played its final night at the Classic on October 20, 1973, before moving on to what became its best known London home, another converted cinema, the 350-seat King's Road Theatre—in the building that once housed the late 1960s countercultural showcase the Essoldo, deep within the so evocatively named World's End neighborhood.

There it remained until 1979, perched on a dog's leg in the road that cultural history would later remember better for housing *Seditionaries*, the boutique from which Sex Pistols manager Malcolm McLaren and fashionista Vivienne Westwood later claimed to have blueprinted punk rock. How appropriate that a movement, much less a store, that came to pride itself on its absorption of kink, deviance, and antisociability should also be birthed in the shadow of a play that likewise celebrated all three.

"I think certain elements of punk—for instance, ripped fishnet tights and glitter and the funny colored hair—a lot of those aspects of it were directly attributed to *Rocky*," Sue Blane told authors Scott Michaels and David Evans, and she is correct. For viewers present at the birth of the *Rocky Horror* participation boom, the burgeoning punk rock fashions were little more than an egalitarian adaptation of what the *Rocky* crowd was already wearing.

But McLaren later insisted, "I never gave *Rocky Horror* a second thought. . . . I don't think I was even aware of it." And so its omnipresence has been squeezed out of every halfway definitive history of British punk culture. But that does not mean it was not a part of it; does not mean that the kids who made their way for the first time to McLaren's store did not do so without at least a little prompting from Frank, Magenta, and Riff Raff—all of whom were regular visitors during their time on the King's Road. Indeed, Magenta's shoes and space boots were both purchased there.

Rocky Horror remained in Chelsea until 1979—a quarter of a century beyond the age that it so quintessentially evoked—and then received the news that its latest home too had been marked for the wrecker's ball.

On April 6, 1979, *The Rocky Horror Show* made the final move of its original lifespan, to the 820-seat Comedy Theatre on Panton Street, in London's Leicester Square, the heart, at last, of the capital's West End theater district. There the show finally stepped into the realm of traditional theater—for the first time in its six-year run, it played out on a proscenium stage; for the first time too the action took place *before* the audience, as opposed to occasionally within it. At the Kings' Road Theatre, for instance, Frank-N-Furter made his entrance from behind the audience; now he was forced to enter from the stage, if only for the benefit of audience members watching from the dress and upper circles of the three-level theater.

The Rocky Horror Show remained at the Comedy until September 13, 1980, finally closing after an impressive run of 2,960 performances.

CHAPTER 4

This Decadence Saps Our Wills

The Rocky Horror Show had been onstage for less than six months when it was first suggested that it become a movie, a notion spawned by American record and movie producer Lou Adler. Already an established figure in the U.S. music industry, with movie credits that dated back to the 1967 filming of the Monterey Pop Festival, Adler was introduced to the play by his then girlfriend, actress Britt Ekland, herself an already long-standing supporter of the show.

Adler's suggestion did not immediately set O'Brien's world aflame. "When someone suggested we do *Rocky* as a film, I just went along for the ride," he confessed. "I said, 'Oh yeah, sure.' I was very casual about the whole thing. It seemed quite surreal to me. I never went home and said,

'Wow! We're going to make a movie!' I've thought about it since though and said, 'Wow! We *made* a movie!' The strange thing is that *Rocky* is a parody of the cinema for stage, so actually putting it on film was a bit disorienting. Were we reverting to the original, the thing that was being parodied? Or was it a comment upon a comment upon a comment?"

It was Adler too who suggested to Michael White that the play be transferred to Los Angeles, as the first step toward securing the interest of a major Hollywood movie studio. He already knew which one he wanted to bring on board: 20th Century Fox. Retaining Tim Curry alone from the London production, Adler booked *The Rocky Horror Show* into his own 500-seat Roxy Theatre in Hollywood.

Two previews prepared Los Angeles for the production; then *The Rocky Horror Show* finally premiered in the United States on March 21, 1974. Onstage, Curry stepped out along-side a new all-American cast comprising Meat Loaf in the dual roles of Eddie and Dr. Scott, Kim Milford as Rocky, Bruce Scott as Riff Raff, Boni Enten as Columbia, Jamie Donnelly as Magenta and the Usherette (named Trixie for the first time; in London, she was known as Miss Strawberry Time), Bill Miller as Brad, Abigale Haness as Janet, and Graham Jarvis as the Narrator.

But no less than in London, *Rocky Horror* stepped onto fertile ground. Hollywood was home to many of the movies it referenced; though critically and commercially reviled, the B movies of the past were a part of the landscape, and a part of the pop cultural landscape too. Former Beatle Ringo Starr's latest LP, *Goodnight Vienna*, had just been released with its cover photo drawn directly from *The Day the Earth Stood Still*, set atop the distinctively platter-piled Capitol Records building on Hollywood and Vine; Frank Zappa was joking to concert audiences about his recollections of the movie *Mars Needs Women*. And of course, L.A. has always taken a freak show to its heart.

The Rocky Horror Show would remain in Los Angeles for nine months, playing until January 5, 1975. Behind the scenes, however, things were moving fast. As soon as he was certain the play was the success he had envisioned, Adler invited 20th Century Fox head Gordon Stulberg to the Roxy to see it. A specially invited audience of *Rocky Horror*'s most vociferous local fans was recruited and, while Adler later admitted that he never did discover if Stulberg truly understood what he was watching, he certainly understood enthusiasm. And this audience was wild.

A deal was struck within days; a budget in the region of a million dollars was allocated to the production—small change even by the standards of the time. But that would not change the devotion of the cast and crew, or the ultimate magic of the movie itself.

From the very outset, it made sense to cast as many of the play's original company as was possible—Curry, O'Brien, Quinn, Little Nell, and Adams from the 1973 London production; Meat Loaf from the Los Angeles run. In addition, director Jim Sharman and stage and costume designers Brian Thomson and Sue Blane were recalled to the film set, the latter very much against her better judgment, at least to begin with.

"I remember waking up one morning and saying, 'Oh, I really don't want to do this movie. I really have had enough.' I'd been involved with *Rocky* for quite a long time by then and was getting scared that that was all I was ever going to do. It was also getting embarrassing when you ran into someone on the street and they'd ask, 'What are you doing?' And I'd have to say, 'I'm still doing *Rocky.*' Luckily I've gotten over that now."

Sharman too was initially undecided, and even after he agreed to come on board, there were still decisions to be made. "When Lou Adler and Michael White, the original producers, first invited me to direct the film, they gave me two options. One was a regular movie musical budget and schedule, with the proviso that I cast some established stars—current rock stars, movie stars, whatever; and the other was an essentially B picture budget and a short six week schedule, if I stayed with key members of the original cast and creative team. *Rocky Horror* had flouted conventional wisdom from the get-go and the B picture route seemed truer to its spirit.

"That spirit was something I wanted to keep alive in the film—more spirit than polish was both the aim and the outcome. There was also a strong sense of camaraderie and like-mindedness amongst the original creative team, so I chose option B and that pretty much governed everything that followed—it created the best and the worst. I'm still grateful that Lou and Michael understood this, and went with it."

On another occasion, Sharman reflected, "Insisting on staying with the original cast for Frank and his trio of servants—Tim, Richard, Pat, and Nell—and to keep the original designers—Brian Thomson and Sue Blane—was part of staying true to the source."

Yet there were some surprise inclusions too. Pierre La Roche, one of theater and rock music's most talented make-up artists, was brought in to handle the cast's visual appearance; photographer Mick Rock, likewise a legend in rock circles, was hired to preserve it for the publicity photographs. And in front of the cameras, the young Susan Sarandon (Janet) and Barry Bostwick (Brad) were introduced to add some wholesome American blood to the production, with both slipping effortlessly into the roles of the virginal ingénues suddenly caught up in Frank-N-Furter's web of intrigue and depravity.

It is often alleged that the two Americans were cast at 20th Century Fox's insistence—that the movie studio heads believed (and may well have been correct) that a movie could never break big in America unless there were a few Americans in it.

Jim Sharman, however, is adamant that he had no idea whether such a stipulation was ever made. "I knew the casting would be central to the film's success, and it's obviously been at the heart of its late-night appeal. To me, the house is haunted Europe and the naïve arrivals, Brad and Janet, are from the new world. It was logical to have real Americans play these roles and we were fortunate to find Susan Sarandon and Barry Bostwick at the very beginning of their careers."

In fact, both Bostwick and Sarandon were already confirmed fans of the play, having seen it during its Los Angeles run; Sarandon had befriended Curry as well, and it was while she was visiting him at the Roxy one day that she was first offered a role in the movie.

The casting of Bostwick was very much the box office coup. Born on February 24, 1945 in San Mateo, California; a graduate of the California Western University School of Arts, where he studied for an acting degree; and having done graduate work at the New York University School of the Arts, Bostwick was twenty-two when he made his stage debut in a production of *Take Her, She's Mine*. Two years later, in 1969, he made his Broadway debut in *Cock-a-Doodle Dandy*, but it was his portrayal of Danny Zuko (the role that John Travolta took in the subsequent movie) in the 1972 musical *Grease* that established his name, even earning him a Tony nomination. He was also making his name in movies when *Rocky Horror* came calling, with roles in both *Road Movie* (1974) and *The Wrong Damn Film* (1975), but this was to be a very different part for him to play.

Sarandon too was already a known name, albeit in a career that she had never really planned for. The wife of actor Chris Sarandon, Susan Tomalin was born on October 4, 1946, in New York City. She studied to be a dancer, and she and her husband had just graduated Catholic University in Washington when they answered a casting call for the new John G. Avilsden movie *Joe*.

Chris, who was already an experienced actor, was passed over; his wife, who admitted that "a career isn't that important to me," was handed the role of the leading character's daughter. An impressive debut, it kick-started a career in both television and cinema; by the time she was cast in *The Rocky Horror Picture Show* in 1974, Sarandon was already familiar from memorable roles in such soaps as *Search for Tomorrow*, the short-lived *A World Apart*, and *Lady Liberty*, and movies *The Front Page* (with Jack Lemmon and Walter

Matthau) and *Lovin' Molly* (alongside Anthony Perkins). She arrived in England fresh from costarring with Robert Redford in *The Great Waldo Pepper*, and it was these experiences that she drew upon for her role as Janet Weiss. "You know when I did *The Rocky Horror Show*, I was making fun of every ingénue that I had ever played."

Peter Hinwood, cast as Rocky, also brought the movie a new dimension, as well as a moment of beautiful serendipity. His first major scene in the movie, his birth, was fittingly shot on October 30—the eighty-first birthday of Charles Atlas, the bodybuilding legend who originally spoke the words "In just seven days, I can make you a man."

Born on May 17, 1946, Hinwood worked as both a photographer and a professional model in between acting jobs . . . which were few and far between, but certainly notable. He appeared as the Hellenic God Hermes in British TV's late-1960s series *The Adventures of Ulysses*, and also had a role alongside Ava Gardner in Roddy McDowall's first and only directorial effort, *The Ballad of Tam Lin*. He would not, however, pursue his acting career. "One, I can't act," he told *People* magazine. "Two, I cringe with embarrassment every time I see myself on film. Three, I relish a quiet, peaceful life."

The last of the movie's major players was Charles Gray as the Criminologist. Gray arrived already firmly established as one of British film's most recognizable character actors and still trailing the aura of, contrarily, a criminal mastermind—in 1971, he appeared as Ernst Stavro Blofeld in the James Bond movie *Diamonds Are Forever*. Prior to that, he was the charismatically evil head of a satanic cult, the singularly named Mocata, in Hammer's phenomenal staging of the Dennis Wheatley occult thriller *The Devil Rides Out*, a role that even Hammer's critics (and there have been many over the years) describe as one of this magnificent actor's finest ever performances.

It was to the entire production's credit and good fortune that Gray was able to bring the same combination of charm and menace to *Rocky Horror*, although it is said that when he was offered the role of the criminologist, he simply smiled and asked, "Why not?"

"I never expected to be the object of a cult," Gray said with laughter years later, insisting that he had never even been to see *The Rocky Horror Picture Show*. "I never see any of my films. [So] it's quite a shock, all the madness that's erupted around the whole *Rocky Horror* phenomenon. Sal Piro, the president of the *Rocky Horror* Fan Club, has the coat I wore in that film and he lends it out on special occasions. It's a sort of relic. Like I am."

Of all the movie's stars, however, it is the distinctively framed Meat Loaf to whom hindsight perhaps awards the greatest role, as he bridged the void between a hitherto underachieving career on the fringes of the music industry with his emergence, in 1977, as the voice behind the mega-selling *Bat Out of Hell* album.

Meat Loaf was born Marvin Lee Aday in Dallas, Texas, and relocated to Los Angeles following his mother's death in 1965. There he formed his first band, Meat Loaf Soul, and, according to legend, cleared the club at his very first gig . . . when the smoke machine malfunctioned.

Over the next few years, the band became a staple on the local scene, often being called in as the opening act for various visiting superstars but never enjoying more than regional success; a single, "Once Upon a Time," sold poorly, and Meat Loaf once admitted that the greatest struggle he ever faced was the battle to be taken seriously. In an age when rock stars were svelte, the jumbo-sized Loaf completely bucked the trend. One critic looked back and recalled him as "the male Mama Cass"; Meat Loaf himself likened his treatment to that of a circus clown.

A role in the Los Angeles production of *Hair* did much to lift Meat Loaf out of this rut, and in 1971, he and another *Hair* star, Shaun "Stoney" Murphy, were signed to the Motown label to cut an album, *Stoney and MeatLoaf*, and a minor hit single, "What You See Is What You Get."

Still his musical career was stalled, and Meat Loaf returned to the stage, this time for the Broadway production of *Hair*. From there, he moved on to the Public Theater's antiwar production *More Than You Deserve*, where he first encountered songwriter Jim Steinman, his partner in the *Bat Out of Hell* experience. Other appearances included *As You Like It* with Raul Julia and, in late 1973, a short production of *Rainbow in New York* in Washington, D.C. It was then that he received the call for the L.A. production of *The Rocky Horror Show*, where he made such a splash that he not only was called back for the movie but also wound up responsible for the supporting feature when the finished movie went out to the theaters. At the same time as he was filming, Meat Loaf was also scheming *Bat Out of Hell* with Jim Steinman, recording songs and—half a decade before the practice became an industry standard—shooting accompanying videos. He showed one of these, "Paradise by the Dashboard Light," to Lou Adler, who promptly agreed to send it out with the film.

Casting for the movie was all but complete by early September 1974; that same month, Curry and Meat Loaf took their leave of the Los Angeles stage and returned to London to begin recording the movie soundtrack. (Their roles were taken over by Paul Jabara and Alan Martin respectively.) At the legendary Olympic Studios in Barnes, where acts as far apart as the Stones, Led Zeppelin, and Jimi Hendrix had all recorded, musical director Richard Hartley assembled a band that included a couple of members of the rock band Procol Harum and session keyboard player John "Rabbit" Bundrick of Traffic. Also on the session was Clare Torry, one of Britain's best loved backing vocalists and an integral part of the Pink Floyd sound—those are her ethereal tones that give the *Dark Side of the Moon* LP so much of its emotional punch.

With such a crew on hand, the backing tracks were complete within just four days.

Filming of *The Rocky Horror Picture Show* then got under way on October 21, 1974, at Bray Studios in Maidenhead, just outside of London. It was an appropriate venue. Bray was home to some of the most popular (and, perhaps ironically, most reviled) movies in British cinema history, the Hammer series of horror flicks that made stars of Peter Cushing, Christopher Lee, and so many others. Other footage was shot amid the Thames-side beauty of Oakley Court, a startlingly ornate Victorian country house in nearby Windsor, built in 1859, that had likewise seen a great deal of service with Hammer. It had been the headquarters of the French Resistance during World War II, and exiled French leader Charles de Gaulle is said to have spent a night in one of its 118 rooms. A fitting home, then, for an exile from another land . . . another world. Plus, noted Susan Sarandon, laughing, it was haunted "and we made [it] look even more haunted."

The Hammer House of Horror

Although Hammer Films is regarded today as the quintessential British movie producer of the 1950s and 1960s, the studio had actually been around for more than twenty years before 1957's *The Curse of Frankenstein* introduced it to the public at large.

As far back as 1932, a Spanish-born movie distributor, Enrique Carreras, and an English vaudeville performer, William Hinds, joined to produce movies under the name of Hammer Films (Hinds had previously been a member of a vaudeville act called Hammer and Smith). Over the next two decades, Hammer produced a string of B movies, concentrating on crime dramas but occasionally branching into other genres—including the spookily effective *The Mystery of the Marie Celeste*. Not until 1955 did the company truly look toward the genre that would establish its name, however, with a movie version of the hugely successful BBC television series *The Quatermass Experiment*.

It proved one of the studio's greatest successes yet, and they began to look for further horror properties, finally seizing upon Mary Shelley's *Frankenstein*—painstakingly reworked and redesigned to avoid any comparison with Universal's 1931 film version, after threats of litigation from the American company's lawyers.

The Curse of Frankenstein emerged in spring 1957, the first British horror movie ever to be shot in color, and the first in what would become a veritable home industry. Dracula, werewolves, and mummies were all exhumed from the horror genre's celluloid past. *Quatermass* returned over the course of two sensational sequels; the legend of the abominable snowman was tapped; so were the Hound of the Baskervilles and the terror of the Chinese *tongs*. Gorgons, reptiles, and witches filed through

Continues on next page

Continued

the Hammer makeup department, as did dinosaurs and devils. Actress Ingrid Pitt created a lesbian vampire queen, Jack the Ripper walked again, and the mad monk, Rasputin, returned to terrorize Moscow society.

Actors the caliber of Raquel Welch, Andrew Keir, Ursula Andress, Diana Dors, Andre Morrell, and Michael Ripper appeared in Hammer movies (some in several), while Peter Cushing and Christopher Lee became synonymous with both the roles they played and the studio for whom they played them. Just as Tim Curry will forever be Frank-N-Furter, no matter how many different roles he's had since *Rocky Horror*, so Lee will always be Count Dracula; Cushing will always be Dr. Frankenstein; and Vincent Price, who made his name in horror both long before and far away from Hammer, but is frequently named in the same breath as the studio—Price simply became *the* personification of horror in all of its cinematic guises, at least in the years before sundry psychotic slashers dislodged him from his pinnacle. (He would attend the first night of *The Rocky Horror Show* in London 1973; two decades later, he would return to the production as its narrator.)

By the early 1970s, Hammer was very much on its last legs. The market for the studio's particular brand of knowingly kitsch horror movies was declining, and the studio responded by returning to the notion that had launched it in the first place: buying up the rights to sundry successful television series and making feature movies of those instead.

This time, however, they opted for the half-hour sitcoms that were dominating the screens—*On the Buses*, revolving around the trials and tribulations of a bus driver; *Nearest and Dearest*, and *Love Thy Neighbour*. In 1974, as the cameras rolled on *Rocky Horror*, Hammer had just one movie awaiting release, a full-length version of the sitcom *Man About the House* (the UK prototype for American TV's *Three's Company*). An era had ended—but a new one was about to begin.

The influence of Hammer would hang heavy in other ways too. The mood of the movie, far more so than the play, echoes the light-and-shade styling of the classic horror films, and one of *The Rocky Horror Picture Show*'s most iconic moments, the birth of Rocky himself, utilized the same water tank and dummy featured in director Terence Fisher's 1958 production *The Revenge of Frankenstein*. *Rocky Horror*, concluded the fanzine *Cinefantastique*, bore "the unmistakable look of a psychedelic Hammer film."

The movie would not—could not—adhere strictly to the stage show. A number of changes were required for the original scripted production to make the transition to the screen. The wedding scene that is played by ear in the theater was given full presentation. The song "Once in a While" was lost. A number of linking scenes were added for the sake of continuity, and one of the most significant changes was the decision to render Rocky mute, allowing him voice only during the musical numbers—a voice supplied by Australian singer Trevor White (no relation to the similarly named guitarist with the bands Jook and Sparks).

Sharman: "The music for the film was re-arranged by Richard Hartley to suit the musical strengths of the cast. We also rehearsed before we recorded, so the songs were performed with a clear idea of the action involved, allowing the actors to characterize their songs. This resulted in a shift in interpretation between stage and film. For instance: 'Science Fiction' onstage is a chirpy, witty, uptempo song—abrasive and attention demanding. It is, after all, the opening number of a stage show. In the film, it's slow, sinuous and seductive—it draws you in.

"There's a view that the film is just a stage show recorded, but this is far from true. Sometimes, time and budget restraints meant we could only cover the action, but there's more cinematic thinking behind it than is credited. I was influenced by classic German cinema, also stage derived, and this thinking influenced my approach. There's a big difference between the film and stage versions. 'Science Fiction' is an obvious example, but there are plenty more."

One especially contentious move was the decision to have Richard O'Brien sing the opening "Science Fiction/Double Feature" instead of Quinn. "In the stage version, there are usherettes who sing the 'Science Fiction/Double Feature' song, and I played one of those as well as Magenta," Quinn recalled. "So the only reason I agreed to do the movie was to sing the song, not for the actual part of Magenta. So when I asked 'am I singing the song?' they told me 'No,' so I said 'I'm not doing your film.' So then Richard says to me 'You always say no after lunch, Pat, not during it.' I said 'Well, I wanna finish it.'

"So on the last day of shooting Jim Sharman had to find a way to sing the song, so they had O'Brien's voice, who was not as pretty as me. He asked if I had seen the painter/photographer Man Ray's *Lips* and I said 'no,' but have since seen it many times since. He used that picture for his inspiration. This movie was shot on a shoe string budget so they draped some material on the camera. In order to keep my head from moving, they screwed it into an art lamp that had been sitting on the stage, this made me look like Frankenstein."

One of the most distinctive openings in cinema history was created.

Yet the movie also suffered its own succession of cuts and changes. Plans for the film to open in black and white, burst into widescreen for the "Time Warp" scene, and then explode into Technicolor when Frank makes his debut were revised during the final production phase (the original footage can be found as an Easter egg on the twenty-fifth anniversary DVD). Hopes that "Science Fiction/Double Feature" could be accompanied by clips from the movies it mentions were dashed by the sheer cost and confusion of obtaining the necessary rights and clearances. The film was ultimately shot in the 1.66:1 aspect ratio throughout.

It was an adjustment that Sue Blane, in particular, was unhappy with. She told writer Patricia Morrisroe, "Because the first 20 minutes of the film was supposed to be in black and white, the Transylvanians played a key part in the color switch. Their costumes took a lot of work, and I'm not at all pleased with the results. In the black and white sequence they looked quite proper dressed in their tuxedoes, but when the film went to color you were suddenly supposed to notice that underneath their conventional jackets they were wearing these ridiculously bright shirts. I was hopping it would be a really magic moment. Under the circumstances, it wasn't."

There would be further changes made for international distribution, most notably the decision to cut the song "Superheroes" from the U.S. version. The closing credits too were altered—the UK end credits roll over the "Science Fiction/Double Feature" reprise, the American credits roll over "The Time Warp."

"The version with 'Superheroes' is the original ending and the best one," Sharman explained. "Somewhere, way back when—I guess it was in between the original release and the initial late-night screenings—there was some studio tinkering and 'Superheroes' was deleted, probably through a desire to give it a more conventional movie ending—which is frankly impossible with a film like *The Rocky Horror Picture Show*. The fans eventually complained and the original ending was restored, for which I'm very grateful. I guess there are a few of these older prints still floating around, but the current DVD version is the full original version. The film begins and ends quietly, reflectively, and in darkness—and that's how it should be."

A fully refurbished hotel today, Oakley Court was somewhat dilapidated in 1974, with no reliable heating or basic creature comforts. That, coupled with the unexpectedly damp fall weather that beset southern England that year, conspired to send a number of the cast and crew to the sick bay, not least of all actress Sarandon. She contracted pneumonia and was absent from the set for several days.

Barry Bostwick added his own tale of woe. "The worst thing about the shoot was whenever I had to pee, I'd have to leave the soundstage and go to another building where the bathroom was," he says. "We shot in October, November and December in England. I was always wet. The castle where we shot was leaking. We'd have to walk through a field to get to it." He laughs and adds, "It was a miserable shoot."

Sharman continued, "The schedule was so tight that the film was mostly edited in the camera and our decision to film it at the old Hammer horror studios—which was affordable, but semi-derelict at the time—gave us dire working conditions. I remember everyone freezing in mid-winter and, as we mostly shot in sequence, when we finally got to the underwater filming for 'Don't dream it, be it,' I resorted to encouraging excess by pointing out that the wilder it was, the sooner it would be over! It may look dreamy onscreen, but my only recollection is of chattering teeth and everyone stamping their feet to keep warm while shivering in their underwear."

On another occasion, the studio hosted a delegation of 20th Century Fox movie execs. "[They] were very pleasant but completely baffled by what was going on," Sharman recalled. "They had no frame of reference for this film and the result was they decided to leave us alone and there was no interference. That was probably the best thing that happened, because the finished film is exactly the one we intended to make—spirit intact."

The speed with which the movie was made did create some unintended moments of hilarity. Patricia Quinn recalled, "The movie had a lot of surprises and I didn't know what was going on from day to day. We were at the dinner scene and Tim pulls the cloth off and there is Meat Loaf underneath and everyone screamed because they had no clue he was under there. The movie was made so fast and the crew had no time to talk to the cast."

Despite all this, it was a relatively trouble-free shoot, and principal photography ended on schedule, on December 19, 1974.

After the movie was edited and complete, Adler quickly arranged a screening for the paymasters. They were not impressed. Shot and edited with a deliberate eye for the clunky style of 1950s sci-fi horror kitsch, *The Rocky Horror Picture Show* seemed wholly out of step with the cinematic trends of the time . . . it was the age, after all, of such big-budget behemoths as *Jaws, Rollerball,* and *The Towering Inferno.* What hope did a low-budget musical about spacemen and perverts have against any of them?

None.

And if the studio's doubts were strong, they were only given further credence by the dour news coming out of Broadway.

Having completed that successful Los Angeles run, the production switched coasts, opening at the 967-seat Belasco Theater on March 10, 1975, after an extensive remodeling of the theater. Many of the building's original fittings were dismantled; more, cried Broadway purists, was destroyed, and it would be another thirty-five years before the Belasco was truly restored, for the opening of *Women on the Verge of a Nervous Breakdown.*

The full Roxy cast made the journey, including the returning Tim Curry and Meat Loaf, and there was also a place for Richard O'Brien, taking over the role of Riff Raff after the scheduled performer, Bruce Scott, was injured in another play.

Three previews met with an uncertain response, and matters did not improve. The production closed on April 6, after just forty-five performances, nailed not only by uncomprehending reviews but also by stampeding-the-wrong-way audiences. Anybody who cast an eye across the ocean to where a movie of the same benighted production was already under way must surely have wondered how low it too could sink.

Curry laughed, recalling, "One of the best things that ever happened to me was *Rocky Horror* being a total flop in New York as a play. It was a disaster, and it was the night of the long knives as far as the critics were concerned. And I don't think I've ever really been so unhappy in my whole life, I mean, for your first time on Broadway, to just be taken to the cleaners. . . .

"[I] think that was really one of the most formative things that has ever happened to me. I just went home and took out a bottle of vodka for about a month, actually. It was great—I sent out for submarine sandwiches and drank and got hugely patched, and then started work again. And I think once you've had a really serious failure, nothing can ever be as bad as that again. So you might just as well go for it because they can't make you feel any worse than they did before."

That didn't stop them from trying. *The Rocky Horror Picture Show* opened at the United Artists Theater in Westwood, Los Angeles, on September 26, 1975, and proved an immediate local success. But barely had it hit the national theater circuit than *The Rocky Horror Picture Show* was withdrawn from the eight opening cities due to very small audiences, while its scheduled New York opening, that Halloween, was canceled weeks in advance.

Britain was no less merciless. *The Rocky Horror Picture Show* premiered at the Rialto Theatre on August 14, an event that brought press and onlookers out in force. But Christopher Biggins, playing one of the Transylvanians, told author Scott Michael, "We all came out [of the premiere] and it was like suicide time. You knew the movie was a complete flop when it opened. We went to the premiere and everyone left the theatre wanting to slit their wrists. It was like coming out of a morgue."

An attempt to improve the movie's American reception by sending it out with Brian De Palma's masterful *Phantom of the Paradise* proved equally unsuccessful, for that film too was commercially doomed. Only one pair of influential eyes in the audience, 20th Century Fox's head of advertising, Tim Deegan, saw the movie as anything more than a failed exercise in high camp corniness, especially after he caught the reaction of the nonindustry faces in the audience . . . more fans brought in by the entrepreneurial Adler.

It was in Los Angeles that the cult began, as audiences shifted from curious to besotted; as they began learning favorite lines from the script and developing favored responses to others; as their clothing started to shift to echo that of the characters; as every night, a corner of the auditorium—and an ever-larger corner at that—began to stage its own interpretation of the *Rocky Horror Show*.

Neither, it transpired, was Los Angeles alone in this phenomenon. Elsewhere around the United States, the first reports on *The Rocky Horror Picture Show* claimed that it was barely keeping its head above water. Exhibitor after exhibitor told sad tales of near empty houses at every showing. But although some audiences numbered in mere handfuls, only the most observant people noticed that it was the *same* handful that returned every night. And again, they knew the words, they sang the songs, they walked the walk, and they wore the clothes.

O'Brien confessed that he was astonished by this aspect of the movie's success. "The film runs for 90 minutes just like the show," he said. "But it was a tight hour and a half in the theatre, people picked up the dialogue and it kicked along. When we made the movie it still ran for 90 [actually, it's closer to 100] minutes, but it seemed so slow, there were gaps between lines. And I would watch it and think, 'Why are we hanging around? Those lines should be coming right on top of each other.' Five years later, somebody at a convention asked me if we left the gaps in deliberately so that the audience could put its own dialogue in—and I said, 'Oh yes, that's exactly what that was for.'"

CHAPTER 5

Don't Dream It

Speaking to journalist Patricia Morrisroe in 1979, O'Brien recalled, "While I was in New York I did a few guest appearances. I remember coming out of a radio station one night and seeing several dozen fans doing the 'Time Warp' to a tape. It was quite eerie. The night was very dark and the skyscrapers looked very large and gray and in the middle of this urban landscape you had twenty silent figures, dressed in street clothes, miming the words to 'Time Warp.' It was very weird. Incredible really." And, as for the sense of identification with which fans appeared to view their heroes, he simply laughed.

"They've asked a lot of people to interpret the show's success and they all seem to miss the very obvious answer: It allows the kids to dress up. I see guys on the street in fishnet stockings and corsets and I think it's terrific. It's a major breakthrough. Women have been cross-dressing for years. Now they can wear almost anything, but a man can't. Thanks to *Rocky Horror* a guy can put on fishnets and strut his stuff and feel okay. I see no harm in that at all."

So *that* was the way this movie was going to work, was it?

A few people, whether reviewing or simply commenting upon *The Rocky Horror Picture Show* during its mainstream theatrical release, had suggested that it would have been better screened at a drive-in or placed on the midnight matinee circuit. They were not necessarily being complimentary, but Tim Deegan knew what they meant. Contacting Bill Quigley of the Walter Reade Theater organization in New York City, Deegan outlined an assault on the heart of the city, in the form of an extended midnight matinee run, scheduled to begin at the Waverly Theater on April 1, 1976.

Adler's scheme was simplicity itself. The movie had failed as a major motion picture; it was simply too far off the cultural beaten track to appeal to more than a comparative handful of viewers. But those few weren't simply startlingly loyal and stunningly dedicated. They were also fiercely proprietary. To them, *The Rocky Horror Picture Show* was personal property: a movie that they had discovered by their own diligence; that had not been crammed down their throats by reviews and trailers and wall-to-wall advertising. And Adler, his eye for moviemaking naturally influenced by his experiences in the rock music business, where "cult heroes" were as valued as mainstream successes, was back on firm ground.

Sidestepping any conventional means of advertising the movie's late-night debut, Adler instead worked by pulling out all the stops in terms of promotion, first coining his own increasingly eye-catching slogans and phrases around the major movie hits of the day ("another kind of *Rocky*," referencing the Sylvester Stallone boxing epic; "a different set of *Jaws*," in honor of Steven Spielberg's rampaging shark).

But the point was not to draw people to the theater by hyperbole and advertising. If *The Rocky Horror Picture Show* was to succeed, it would do so by word of mouth; by people going and falling in love, then returning the next week with their friends in tow. Those friends would then bring their friends and, slowly but certainly, a social club would construct itself around the regular ritual of *Rocky Horror*.

"There's no reason to saturate it, to take it away from the people it belongs to," Lou Adler explained in 1979. "I think *Rocky Horror* fans are the happiest people in the world. Every Friday and Saturday night, they have some place to go where they can be with three hundred people they like, and have a good time."

Soon, Adler's own slogans were forgotten as audience members began providing their own comments and quotes, some in letters to the theater's management, others to the journalists who themselves were drawn to the scene by reports of long lines for a late-night movie they had barely even heard of.

"Word of mouth was great," O'Brien explained. "People felt they discovered it themselves and I think that's an element of anything that becomes a cult. I've never defined that before but I think there's truth in what I just said. When you or I discover something, and you think it's just you that's discovered it you go 'oh I've got to introduce you to this.' It becomes our personal journey. It's an individual experience. Millions of people have seen *Rocky Horror* now, but it's still a cult experience. That's the paradox."

The irony was not lost on the movie's cast, either. As Jim Sharman later mused, had *The Rocky Horror Picture Show* run to the studio's original hopes, "after a strong initial release, it would probably have vanished, like other mainstream rock-styled movies of the era. There's something classic about *The Rocky Horror Picture Show* that means it escapes easy categorization, the fans know it—and that's why it's alive today.

"I've often described it as a big home movie, and in that sense it captures a moment in time in a way that has proved curiously timeless. Technically, there's plenty that could be better, but then it wouldn't be what it is, so—no, nothing—*je ne regrette rien.*"

Sharman had returned to his home in Australia following the completion of the movie and relied on the grapevine to keep him apprised of its fate—and its reprieve. Visiting New York soon after, he dropped by the Waverly Cinema and was astonished. "It was in the early days of dress-ups and audience participation and there was great enthusiasm and a sense of anarchic fun in the air—so I really enjoyed it. My strongest memory was that a film which had begun as a celebration of late-night movies had somehow fulfilled its own destiny and entered its own mythology.

"It had become a late-night movie that was being celebrated late-night and I thought that was pretty cool. We had played the original stage show in derelict cinemas and turned them into theaters, and now the film was turning cinemas into theaters—complete with costumes, make-up and audience participation. The fact that the film had become wallpaper for a non-stop party didn't bother me at all—I thought it was great that the movie was generating so much energy and pleasure."

The movie was a midnight monster within days of opening, and when the first weeks' reports from New York were collated and sent to exhibitors elsewhere around the country, the news began to spread. Austin, Texas, was the second city to succumb to the picture show; Kansas City, Philadelphia, Baltimore, Dallas, and Phoenix followed. And so did the audiences.

The movie would ultimately run at the Waverly for a record-breaking 95 weeks; within two years, it was making similar midnight waves at more than 50 other theaters around the United States; by the end of the decade, *The Rocky Horror Picture Show* was grossing over $5 million a year, and 20th Century Fox had no less than 200 prints in constant circulation around the country. It is unlikely whether any of the bigger budget blockbusters that had once threatened to wipe it off the map were showing at even a quarter of that.

Barry Bostwick discovered the movie's new life very early on, "when I saw it downtown in New York at . . . I forget the name of the theater. But it was when it was first being discovered, and they started talking back at the screen, you know, and I realized how involved the audience was and how they owned the experience because they wanted to become part of the experience. By being another character in the film, it made the whole sort of theatricalization of it fascinating to me, and it eventually got to the point where you couldn't hear the movie at all. The audience became like the lead . . . and the second lead and the third lead, and everybody was trying to out shout everybody else."

And so it proved. *The Rocky Horror Picture Show* was a commercial flop, exiting the mainstream cinemas as fast as was humanly possible, seemingly to live out the remainder of its sure-to-be-brief lifespan by turning up as a space filler in those establishments that offered all-night movie showings. But there was something about that movie that wouldn't say die; a sense, perhaps, that the people who disliked it were destined to hate it forever—or at least until they forgot about it. But those who liked it would *love* it; more than that, they would fall *in* love with it. And just as nobody is content to spend just one night with the object of their most ardent affection, so *Rocky Horror*'s fans were not happy to simply see it once and then move on.

They returned again and again, in increasing numbers and increasingly bizarre states of dress. It was the L.A. crowd, according to legend, who first started attending showings in the guise of their favorite characters, but the practice spread quickly.

Susan Sarandon attended a performance in 1998. "I took Natalie [Portman] when we were doing *Anywhere But Here*, and my daughter and Lukas Haas and Thora Birch, who was in *Anywhere But Here*, also. The time before that, I took Molly Ringwald when she was eleven or twelve, when we were about to do *The Tempest*." Sarandon attended performances in costume, of course—she always went as Janet Weiss.

By the time the *Rocky Horror* stage show made its (for now) final transfer in London, to the Comedy Theater in the heart of the city's West End in 1979, the UK audience too was in full drag. Today, the weirdos at any stage revival or cinema presentation are the ones who *aren't* decked out in corsets or maid's outfits, 1950s geek chic, or demented butler togs.

Rocky Horror is a lifestyle, and it will never go away. As *New York Rock* put it in 2000, "for those who've never thrown rice at the midnight movie or yelled 'slut!' at a shivering

The *Rocky Horror* Audience Participation Survival Kit

- Bounty bars—to be thrown on the line with "paradise" in it, from a line in a UK commercial for the chocolate and coconut candy bar: "a taste of paradise."
- confetti—to be thrown onstage at the end of the "Charles Atlas Song" reprise.
- flashlights—for added illumination during the "there's a light" chorus of "Over at the Frankenstein Place."
- hot dogs—to be thrown during the line "You're a hot dog and you better not try to hurt her . . . Frankfurter."
- Kit Kats—another candy bar, to be thrown on the line "You get a break" . . . also adapted from a UK TV commercial: "have a break, have a Kit Kat."

celluloid Susan Sarandon, *The Rocky Horror Show* . . . has since transformed into the ultimate cult film."

Jim Sharman: "I always had faith in the originality of the film and felt it would ultimately find its audience, but the early signs weren't good. The fact that it was such an unusual film and that it was devoid of conventional movie stars didn't help. The fashion of the day was for realist films and this was something else. [But] there was a certain crazy logic in the fact that the film would end up turning cinemas into theaters, which is more or less what happened."

- newspaper—for when Janet covers her head to shelter from the rain.
- party poppers, hat, blower—for use and deployment during the dinner/birthday scene and the creation scene.
- playing cards—to be thrown during the line "cards for sorrow, cards for pain."
- rice—to be thrown during the wedding scene at the start.
- rubber gloves—to be snapped along with with Frank-N-Furter during the creation scene.
- toast—to be thrown during the dinner scene.
- toilet paper—yet another UK television reference, to be thrown when Brad exclaims "Great Scott!" upon Dr. Scott's entrance.
- water pistols—to re-create the rainstorm that sends Brad and Janet to the castle in the first place.

Sadly, several of these practices have since been discouraged by theaters, due to health and safety concerns.

CHAPTER 6

Rocky Horror—the Second (at Least) Coming

The Rocky Horror Show has never been retired; nor has its popularity ever diminished, either as a crowd pleaser or in terms of its original cast and creator's careers. Even Tim Curry, whose own work has extended across a wealth of movies and stage performances (most recently the Broadway production of Eric Idle's *Spamalot*), knows that he owes much of his popularity to a role he created at the outset of his career; although Richard O'Brien surely spoke for everybody involved when he told writer Dominick A. Miserandino in 1999, "Well, when you do something like *Rocky* which is indefinable somehow, it always becomes difficult to lose that. Not that I have any interest in saying goodbye to *Rocky*. I absolutely adore being involved and a part of something that is really a phenomenon.

"With the film around for 25 years and the show being around even longer—still running and continuing to fill houses all around the world—it's really an exciting and wonderful thing to be part of that. And I have no problems with that at all. If it all overshadows anything else, I can understand completely why and again it doesn't worry me."

The first indication that *Rocky Horror was* going to overshadow much of what its creators did next came in 1981, with the release of *Shock Treatment*, a Richard O'Brien movie intended to tell the continuing story of Brad (Cliff De Young) and Janet (Jessica Harper—coincidentally, the star of the original film's first-run theatrical partner, *Phantom of the Paradise*) in the years following their marriage.

The follow-up was originally intended as a direct sequel, to be titled *Rocky Horror Shows His Heels*, but the unavailability of Tim Curry put the kibosh on that idea, leading O'Brien to explore other notions—*The Brad and Janet Show* and finally *Shock Treatment*. O'Brien, Patricia Quinn, Charles Gray, and Nell Campbell all reappeared, albeit as different characters; only one member of the original team, Jeremy Newson, was cast in his original role, that of Ralph Hapschatt. In addition, director and coauthor Sharman, musical director Richard Hartley, designer Brian Thomson, costumer Sue Blane, and executive producers Lou Adler and Michael White all returned to the scene of the crime. But there, all concerned were adamant, the comparisons ended. "It's not a sequel . . . it's not a prequel . . . it's an equal," producer John Goldstone insisted.

Set back in Denton, the scene of the original movie, *Shock Treatment*'s underlying theme was what O'Brien perceived as the modern world's obsession with television, illustrated by the entire town having been transformed into a giant TV studio, in which the residents lived their lives according to the scripting and characterization of whichever show they happened to be in.

Into this insanity arrive Brad and Janet, still as guileless and innocent as they were when last we saw them, the latest contestants in a daytime marriage-counseling show called *Marriage Maze*, ringmastered by the larger-than-life host Bert Schnick (played by Australian comic Barry Humphries). Unfortunately, the show is not what it seems to be, as they instead find themselves ensnared in the machinations of the show's sponsor, fast-food tycoon Farley Flavors, whose attempts to win Janet for himself stop at nothing—including having Brad committed to the town's insane asylum, run by two psychiatrists who are even madder than their patients, Cosmo and Nation McKinley (Richard O'Brien and Patricia Quinn), and a head nurse, Ansalong (Little Nell), who is as endearingly squeaky as she ever was in the first film.

"The intentions of the two films are quite disparate," director Sharman declared, "the only tangible links being Brad and Janet as catalyst to the plot. *Shock Treatment* shows a cartoon world of television-influenced lifestyles and media manipulation by presenting our TV images, situations, and characters trying to avoid reality. Rather, we're giving a new perspective on what is served up every day by the media as reality."

"We always knew there would be a follow-up to *The Rocky Horror Picture Show*," O'Brien revealed. "There's always a *Son of . . .* , a *Bride of . . .* and a *Son of . . . Rides Again*. But we wanted to do something totally different. When we initially conceived *Shock Treatment*, Brad and Janet's home was a real place. The Dentonvale sanitarium was real. Everything was real. The film was set in an American suburb and we were going to shoot as much as we could on location in the USA.

"But then the Screen Actors strike intervened—and it turned out to be a stroke of good luck. We had to film the picture in England, but since we couldn't recreate American locations there, the movie had to be shot in a studio. It was then that we came up with the idea of setting the whole production inside a TV studio, and making the entire film look like it was shot off a television soundstage. The story is exactly the one we started out with, but the framework and 'live theatre' look of the film is new."

For all its promise, the brilliance of its soundtrack, and the sheer mayhem of the movie itself, *Shock Treatment* shockingly came and went with very little attention, even from the *Rocky Horror* devotees—perhaps because of its nonsequel nature. "I don't think you can repeat [the impact of the original film]," Barry Bostwick mused years later. "I mean, look at the sequel. What was that called? *Shock Treatment*. I never saw that, but it was a miserable failure . . . even more of one than *Rocky Horror* was when it first came out! That one wasn't even re-discovered and turned into a cult hit."

Sal Piro of the *Rocky Horror* fan club (and host of a simultaneous documentary, *The Rocky Horror Treatment*) continued, "As with *Rocky*, this film was tested in a few markets. This was not a movie that could run weekday afternoon shows in a suburban mall and so it was not widely released. It did, however, get spot midnight bookings around the country, and on a few occasions, ran on a double bill with *Rocky Horror*.

"In New York City, while we were firmly implanted at the 8th Street Playhouse, *Shock Treatment* was booked Friday and Saturday nights at our old home, the Waverly, just a few blocks away. *Shock Treatment* did develop its own floor show and audience participation by a group of fringe people from the 8th Street Playhouse. They were not very successful and came under much criticism (especially in an article in the

Village Voice), by those who said that their participation was forced and not like *Rocky Horror*."

Chastened, perhaps, by the movie's reception, the creators have made no concrete attempt to follow up either the stage show or the movie since that time. Plans for a bona fide sequel, *Revenge of the Old Queen*, focusing on Riff Raff's return to Earth, were scrapped despite producer Michael White returning to the team; a late-2000s attempt by MTV Films and Sky Movies to simply remake the original, without any input from O'Brien himself, seems to have petered out somewhere between conception and the realization that it really wasn't a very good idea. But Ryan Murphy, creator of Fox TV's *Glee*, has spoken longingly of the possibility of remaking the movie, even posting a declaration of his intent with the broadcast, on October 26, 2010, of *The Rocky Horror Glee Show*—the ghastly cast of that show's own brief homage to the original.

"What a waste of money," Barry Bostwick sniffed. "It would be like saying, 'Hey, let's go remake *Casablanca*! How are you going to remake it? Every time it was done on stage, I thought it showed the flaws of the piece. I think it's a one-off; I mean, I don't know. You should just leave those things alone. I think films like [*Rocky Horror*] are stand-alones, and they're brilliant for what they were at the time they were done. I mean, you would have to do it as a period piece. It's not like you're going to update *Oklahoma!* It's of its time."

If television and film seem only to want to update or upstage the original *Rocky Horror Show*, however, the theater has remained reassuringly true to its roots, and has been rewarded accordingly.

No matter that the 1975 Broadway adaptation failed. Five years later, emboldened by the underground success of the movie, a new production toured the United States, to be followed, four years later, by a new production in the UK by the Theatre Royal, Hanley. Revivals and tours of its British, American, and Australian strongholds have continued ever since. A wealth of foreign-language productions have also been staged, including several that are now considered theatrical landmarks in their countries of origin.

Perhaps the most significant revival of them all, however, was the $3.5 million production that ran between October 2000 and January 2002 at the Circle in the Square Theatre on Broadway. Featuring Tom Hewitt (later Terrence Mann) as Frank-N-Furter, Alice Ripley as Janet, Raúl Esparza (later Sebastian Bach) as Riff Raff, Joan Jett as Columbia/Usherette (later Ana Gasteyer), Lea DeLaria (later Jason Wooten) as Eddie/Dr. Scott, Daphne Rubin-Vega as Magenta, and Dick Cavett as the Narrator, the revival was nominated for the following Tony Awards: Best Actor: Tom Hewitt; Best Costume

Designer: David C. Woolard; Best Director: Christopher Ashley; and Best Musical Revival.

Of the cast, the inclusion of rocker Joan Jett was perhaps the most surprising, although she quickly revealed that she had been among the movie's greatest supporters during its time in Los Angeles. "Me and my friends would go to see it all the time," she recalled. "We went a lot."

Since that time, she had homaged the opening lips sequence from *The Rocky Horror Show* in the video for her single "The French Song"; but twenty-five years had passed since Joan and her friends had made a point of catching every screening of *The Rocky Horror Picture Show*, learning every line of dialogue and cheering or hooting the action as it unfolded; twenty-five years too since the first New York production of *Rocky Horror* fell so flat on Broadway. Director Christopher Ashley admitted that they were taking a chance with the revival.

"When the play and the film came out in the early '70s, a guy putting on a dress was really cutting edge," he explained. But thirty years later, "how many times have you seen RuPaul on network television?"

Jett's audition was smooth sailing; she probably knew most of her lines by heart, anyway, after so many years of watching and rewatching the movie. She was asked to read the scene where Frank-N-Furter's cruelty finally causes

Columbia to snap; then she was called back to try out with a choreographer, to make certain that she was able to follow direction.

She could, but it was frustrating work. "I've never danced," she admitted to writer Mary Campbell. "I'm a perfectionist. I expected to get the dance steps right the first time." Still she grasped the role, and now she was plunged into some of the most intensive rehearsals of her entire career. "It's been pretty demanding," she understated at the time. "I'm pretty sore and tired, and trying to catch up on sleep and stuff."

Some revisions were made. Writing the play back in the early 1970s, Richard O'Brien gave the character of Columbia a tap-dancing sequence, as a reminder of when he'd been asked to portray a tap-dancing King Herod in *Jesus Christ Superstar*. Would Jett too be forced to sublimate her rocker persona for the joys of tap?

Would she, hell. Instead, she grabbed a convenient guitar and soloed the guts out of it, a moment the watching *Entertainment Weekly* proclaimed the highlight of her entire performance. "Jett never quite adapts her proto-riot grrrl rock persona to the role of Columbia, if only because she's not trained for this kind of stage. [But] when she plugs in a guitar and shreds a few chords, she's on home turf."

A touring British production followed in 2006, borrowing one key aspect of the Broadway version—the use of a revolving narrator. Originally employed on Broadway while the original cast member, Dick Cavett, was on vacation, it has since become a standard feature; the eighteen-month run of the newly retitled *Richard O'Brien's Rocky Horror Show* featured appearances from Michael Aspel, Nigel Planer, Clive Mantle, Russ Abbot, Steve Pemberton, John McArdle, Roger Lloyd-Pack, Ian Lavender, Shaun Williamson, Andy Gray, Jack Ellis, Brian Capron, Russell Grant, and one member of the original movie cast, Christopher Biggins—who, as a struggling unknown thirty years earlier, had appeared as one of the Transylvanians.

The 2006 tour was directed by Christopher Luscombe and featured David Bedella as Frank-N-Furter, Suzanne Shaw as Janet, Matthew Cole as Brad, Iain Davey as Riff Raff, Shona White as The Usherette/Magenta, Kay Murphy as Columbia, Julian Essex-Spurrier as Rocky, and Nathan Amzi as Eddie/Dr. Scott, with Sarah Boulton, Stuart Ellis, Lynden O'Neill, and Claire Parrish as the newly conceived Phantoms. An almost totally different cast then stepped in following the play's Christmas season at the Comedy Theatre, London: Richard Meek as Brad, Sarah Boulton and later Hayley Tamaddon as Janet, Matt Harrop as Riff Raff, Claire Parrish as The Usherette/Magenta, Sarah French-Ellis and later Sarah Boulton as Columbia, and Sergio Priftis as Rocky, with Lauren Appleby, Erin Carter, and Kevin Littlejohn as the Phantoms.

Luscombe then created a successful revival in 2009, another year-plus venture that kicked off on September 17, 2009, at the New Wimbledon Theatre. With David Bedella again appearing as Frank-N-Furter and Nathan Amzi and Stuart Ellis returning, respectively, as Eddie/Dr. Scott and Phantom, the 2009 revival also featured Richard Meek as Brad, Haley Flaherty as Janet, Brian McCann as Riff Raff, Kara Lane as The Usherette/Magenta, Ceris Hine as Columbia, and Dominic Tribuzio as Rocky.

And there is more, as Rocky got raunchy in 2011 for Wicked Pictures' wicked porn parody, *The Rocki Whore Picture Show*. This was by no means the first attempt to eroticize the original movie, although even porno fans apparently squirm at the mention of such low-budget predecessors as *The Rocky Porno Video Show* (1986) and *Funky Fetish Horror Show* (2002).

This time, however, everything came together in perfect harmony. Thrill as Brad (Rocco Reed) and Janet (Jessica Drake) get down and dirty on the wedding night in a stalled car; as they make their way through a raging storm to the sinister castle where legendary director Frank 'n' Beans (Mac Turner) is about to make the greatest porno film ever; as they encounter Vagina (Nicki Hunter), the maid, and Stiff Staff (Randy Spears), the handyman; and as Frank unveils his most breathtaking creation, the ultimate porn actress, the titular Miss Whore.

Of course it is silly, of course it is shocking, and of course many fans of the original will scream sacrilege and dismiss it as disgusting. Others, however, adore it. With director Brad Armstrong having reached out to the world of fandom, many of the costumes and props employed in the movie came from theatrical productions of the original play, and there were also hopes that Patricia Quinn would voice the opening theme song. "We went back and forth with her," Armstrong told *Adult Video News* magazine, "but she knows the *Rocky* people will get all pissed off."

Armstrong shoots with unabashed love for the original production, the cast do their level best to be instantly recognizable (Turner, in particular, parodies Tim Curry to electrifying effect); and there is even a handful of musical tributes straight out of the Richard O'Brien songbook, with only lyrics and titles changed to protect the innocent.

It is a raw and raucous romp, a vision that seizes upon the sexual undercurrents that swirled through the original and brings them squirming and squelching to the surface, a revival that revitalizes parts that other versions of the story are way too polite to realize.

And yet . . .

And yet, although we use the word "revival" so naturally in this regard, and treat every fresh production as another thread in the vast tapestry that is *Rocky Horror*, are we not also a little disingenuous—to ourselves, to the concept, to Rocky himself?

For how can you truly revive something that has never gone away?

For close to four decades—again, *Rocky Horror* will be forty in 2013—*The Rocky Horror Show* has been a constant force in, and on, the lives of more people than could ever be counted.

From the original cast, so unwittingly stepping out on that tiny stage in 1973, uncertain whether people would even understand, let alone enjoy, what they were about to enact; through to the burgeoning crowds that answered that question over the next few weeks . . . through the overseas productions that have seen *Rocky Horror* circumnavigate the globe . . . the crew and cast who made the movie, the crowds who flocked and frolicked in *its* shadow . . . and on, now, to *you*, reading this book and adding your own thoughts and theories to the universal Rocky consciousness, *Rocky Horror* has established itself as perhaps *the* defining countercultural icon of the late twentieth and early twenty-first centuries.

And it did so, as the Beatles almost put it, with nothing more than a little help from its friends.

We are all Superheroes.

THE RECORDINGS

The following cast recordings have been made available worldwide since 1973:

1973 London Cast
1974 Roxy Cast
1974 Australian Cast
1975 Brazilian Cast
1975 Film Soundtrack
1976 Mexican Cast
1977 Norwegian Cast
1978 New Zealand Cast (starring Gary Glitter; directed by
    Rayner Bourton)
1980 German Cast
1981 Australian Cast
1990 London Cast ("The Whole Gory Story")

1991 Icelandic Cast

1992 Australian Cast

1994 German Cast

1995 New Zealand Cast

1995 Finnish Cast

1995 Icelandic Cast

1995 German Cast

1996 Danish Cast

1996–97 European Tour

1997 German Cast

1998 London Cast

1998 South African Cast

2001 Broadway Cast

2001 Korean Cast

2001 Peruvian Cast

2002 Philippine Cast

2005 Vancouver Cast

2007 Panamanian Cast

2009 Mexican Cast

The following songs were performed at the original run of the Rocky Horror Show at the Theatre Upstairs at The Royal Court (1973):

"Science Fiction/Double Feature"

"Dammit, Janet!"

"Over at the Frankenstein Place"

"Sweet Transvestite"

"The Time Warp"

"The Sword of Damocles"

"Hot Patootie"

"Touch-a, Touch-a, Touch-a, Touch Me"

"Once in a While"

"Planet Schmanet Janet"

"Rose Tint My World/Don't Dream It, Be It/Wild and Untamed Thing"

"I'm Going Home"

"Superheroes"

"Science Fiction/Double Feature (Reprise)"

Performed at Classic Cinema and King's Road Theatre (formerly the Essoldo Cinema) (1973–1979)

"Science Fiction/Double Feature"

"Dammit, Janet!"

"Over at the Frankenstein Place"

"Sweet Transvestite"

"The Time Warp"

"The Sword of Damocles"

"I Can Make You a Man"

"Hot Patootie—Bless My Soul"

"I Can Make You a Man (Reprise)"

"Touch-a, Touch-a, Touch-a, Touch Me"

"Once in a While"

"Eddie's Teddy"*

"Planet Schmanet Janet"

"Rose Tint My World/Don't Dream It, Be It/Wild and Untamed Thing"

"I'm Going Home"

"Superheroes"

"Science Fiction/Double Feature (Reprise)"

Comedy Theatre (1979–1980)

ACT I

"Science Fiction/Double Feature"

"Dammit, Janet!"

"Over at the Frankenstein Place"

"Sweet Transvestite"

"The Time Warp"

"The Sword of Damocles"

"I Can Make You a Man"

---

* Until the release of the Roxy cast album, the only officially available recording of "Eddie's Teddy" was on the B-side of the 1975 single "Merry Christmas Baby" by Kimi and Ritz.

"Hot Patootie—Bless My Soul"
"I Can Make You a Man (Reprise)"

ACT II

"Touch-a, Touch-a, Touch-a, Touch Me"
"Once in a While"
"Eddie's Teddy"
"Planet Schmanet Janet"
"Rose Tint My World"
"Don't Dream It, Be It"
"Wild and Untamed Thing"
"I'm Going Home"
"Superheroes"
"Science Fiction/Double Feature (Reprise)"

THE CREDITS

The Cast—London

ORIGINAL LONDON CAST

Patricia Quinn as Usherette/Magenta

Julie Covington as Janet Weiss (replaced by Belinda Sinclair)

Christopher Malcolm as Brad Majors

Jonathan Adams as Narrator

Richard O'Brien as Riff Raff

Little Nell as Columbia

Tim Curry as Frank-N-Furter

Rayner Bourton as Rocky

Paddy O'Hagan as Eddie/Dr. Everett Scott

CLASSIC CINEMA

Patricia Quinn as Usherette/Magenta (replaced by Angela Bruce)

Belinda Sinclair as Janet Weiss

Christopher Malcolm as Brad Majors (replaced by James Warwick)

Jonathan Adams as Narrator

Richard O'Brien as Riff Raff

Little Nell as Columbia

Tim Curry as Frank-N-Furter

Rayner Bourton as Rocky

Paddy O'Hagan as Eddie/Dr. Everett Scott

KING'S ROAD THEATRE

Angela Bruce as Usherette/Magenta

Belinda Sinclair as Janet Weiss

James Warwick as Brad Majors (replaced by James Warwick)

Jonathan Adams as Narrator

Richard O'Brien as Riff Raff

Little Nell as Columbia

Tim Curry as Frank-N-Furter (replaced by Philip Sayer)

Philip Sayer as Frank-N-Furter (replaced by Ziggy Byfield)

Rayner Bourton as Rocky

Paddy O'Hagan as Eddie/Dr. Everett Scott

Film Credits

CAST

Tim Curry . . . Dr. Frank-N-Furter—A Scientist

Susan Sarandon . . . Janet Weiss—A Heroine

Barry Bostwick . . . Brad Majors—A Hero

Richard O'Brien . . . Riff Raff—A Handyman

Patricia Quinn . . . Magenta—A Domestic

Nell Campbell (as Little Nell) . . . Columbia—A Groupie

Jonathan Adams . . . Dr. Everett V. Scott—A Rival Scientist

Peter Hinwood . . . Rocky Horror—A Creation

Meat Loaf . . . Eddie—Ex Delivery Boy

Charles Gray . . . The Criminologist—An Expert

Jeremy Newson . . . Ralph Hapschatt

Hilary Labow . . . Betty Munroe Hapschatt

John Marquand . . . Father (uncredited)

Frank Lester . . . Wedding Dad (uncredited)

Petra Leah . . . Bridesmaid (uncredited)

Gina Barrie . . . Bridesmaid (uncredited)

Henry Woolf . . . Wedding Photographer/Transylvanian (uncredited)

Annabel Leventon (as Annabelle Leventon) . . . Transylvanian

Anthony Milner . . . Transylvanian

Christopher Biggins . . . Transylvanian

Fran Fullenwider . . . Transylvanian

Gaye Brown . . . Transylvanian

Hugh Cecil . . . Transylvanian

Imogen Claire . . . Transylvanian

Ishaq Bux . . . Transylvanian

Kimi Wong . . . Transylvanian

Koo Stark . . . Bridesmaid (uncredited)

Lindsay Ingram . . . Transylvanian

Pamela Obermeyer . . . Transylvanian

Peggy Ledger . . . Transylvanian

Perry Bedden . . . Transylvanian

Rufus Collins . . . Transylvanian (uncredited)

Sadie Corre . . . Transylvanian

Stephen Calcutt . . . Transylvanian

Tony Cowan . . . Transylvanian

Tony Then . . . Transylvanian

CREW

Alan Harris—stand-in: Peter Hinwood (uncredited)

B. J. Wilson—principal musician

Barry St. John—background singer (uncredited)

Bill Rowe—dubbing mixer

Bob Douglas—stand-by props (uncredited)

Bob Hedges—stand-by props (uncredited)

Bob Howard—second assistant director (uncredited)

Bob Spencer—scenic artist (uncredited)

Brian Engel—background singer (uncredited)

Bryn Siddall—property buyer (uncredited)

Celestia Fox—casting consultant: UK

Charles Cox—unit driver (uncredited)

Clare Torry—background singer (uncredited)

Colin Chilvers—special effects

Count Ian Blair—principal musician

Dave Murphy—stand-in: Richard O'Brien (uncredited)

Dave Wintour (as David Wintour)—principal musician

David Toguri—choreography

Dennis Lewiston—camera operator

Dick Frift—construction manager

Don Bradburn—dressing props (uncredited)

Doug Smith—sound maintenance (uncredited)

Eric Kent—stand-in: Meat Loaf (uncredited)

Erica Simmons—stand-in: Little Nell (uncredited)

Ernest Gasser—assistant makeup artist (uncredited)

Fred Anderson—electrician (uncredited)

Geoff Freeman—publicist (uncredited)

Gerry Paris—stand-in: Tim Curry (uncredited)

Gillian Dods—wardrobe

Gillian Gregory—assistant choreographer (uncredited)

Graeme Clifford—film editing

Graeme Clifford—music editor

Graham Freeborn—assistant makeup artist (uncredited)

Helen Chapelle—background singer (uncredited)

Helen Lennox—assistant hair stylist (uncredited)

Ian Fuller—dubbing editor

Ian Whittaker—set dresser

Jack Roche—grip (uncredited)

Jane Royle—assistant makeup artist (uncredited)

John Birkinshaw—stand-in: Barry Bostwick (uncredited)

John Bundrick (as Rabbit)—principal musician

John Comfort—production manager

John Goldstone—associate producer

John Jay—still photographer (uncredited)

John Leuenberger—property master (uncredited)

John Siddall—draughtsman (uncredited)

Keith Grant—music recordist

Ken Shepherd—stunt double: Eddie (uncredited)

Len Tremble—assistant dubbing editor (uncredited)

Liz Coke—stand-in: Susan Sarandon (uncredited)

Liza Strike—background singer (uncredited)

Lou Adler—executive producer

Maureen Campbell—accounts secretary (uncredited)

Maureen White—production secretary (uncredited)

Melita Smith—stand-in: Patricia Quinn (uncredited)

Michael White—producer

Mick Grabham—principal musician

Mike Gowans—first assistant director

Mike Lockey—assistant hair stylist (uncredited)

Mike Roberts—camera focus

Nigel Galt—assistant editor (uncredited)

Norman Dorme—assistant art director (uncredited)

Peter Glossop—boom operator (uncredited)

Peter Robb-King—makeup artist

Peter Suschitzky—director of photography

Phil Kenzie—principal musician

Pierre La Roche—original makeup designs creator

Ramon Gow—hairdresser

Richard Hartley—composer: incidental music

Richard O'Brien—composer: original music and lyrics

Richard Pointing—wardrobe

Richard Smith—stand-in: Richard O'Brien (uncredited)

Rodney Glenn—assistant editor

Ron Barron—sound recordist

Ron Swinburne—production accountant

Ronnie Fox Rogers—camera operator: second unit (uncredited)

Roy Spencer—standby special effects (uncredited)

Sue Blane—costume design

Sue Edwards—secretary to producer (uncredited)

Susanna Merre—continuity

Terry Ackland-Snow—art direction

Trevor White—singer (uncredited)

Tuppence Smith—stand-in: Patricia Quinn (uncredited)

Wally Veevers—special effects

ACKNOWLEDGMENTS

Thanks to everybody who helped push this book to completion, and thanks to everyone who ensured I'd want to write it in the first place—Jen, with whom I played Magenta and Riff Raff back when you had to buy their clothes from a junk store; Marion, who should have married Frank-N-Furter; Jo-Ann, who still laughs at the handyman's first line; and Amy, who took to the hills long before *Tarantula* reached them.

NOTES

"I set out to write amusing entertainment": BBC Radio Gloucester, October 2003

"I think Mr Carl Jung might have had something to say about *Rocky*": Celebrity Cafe.com, September 1, 1999

"I truly believe that *Rocky* is an eternal fairytale": Cocklenuggets.blogspot.com, September 26, 2010

"That's why it really works": Cocklenuggets.blogspot.com, September 26, 2010

"it was at the time that the sexual liberation permeated": Scott Michaels and David Evans, *Rocky Horror from Concept to Cult* (London: Sanctuary Books, 2002)

"I was a huge David Bowie": author interview, 2010

"Janet is definitely Little Miss Middle-Class": *Shock Treatment* press release 1981

"I came out of the theater": author interview, 2010

"*Rocky Horror* took everything that was going on in glam rock": author interview, 1986

"I found a crowd of punks and freaks waiting to go in": Gary Glitter with Lloyd Bradley, *The Leader* (London: Ebury Press, 1991)

"Tim Curry's Frank-N-Furter pouting": Barney Hoskyns, *Glam! Bowie, Bolan and the Glitter Rock Revolution* (London: Faber & Faber, 1998)

"a serious blow": Hoskyns, *Glam!*

"My play has no sex preference": quoted by http://www.furious.com/perfect/adultmusicals.html

"New Zealand reminds me very much of the American mid-west": 1979 interview with Patricia Morrisroe, http://www.rockymusic.org/showdoc/RichardOBrien-1979Interview.php

"Though it may seem a big step": The Inaugural Rex Cramphorn Memorial Lecture,

Belvoir Street Theatre, Sydney, July 23, 1995

"Acting was always the important thing in my life": 1979 interview with Patricia Morrisroe, http://www.rockymusic.org/showdoc/RichardOBrien-1979Interview.php

"a way for me to spend": Theatreworld Internet Magazine, 2006

"Writing *Rocky* was almost like working on a jigsaw puzzle": 1979 interview with Patricia Morrisroe, http://www.rockymusic.org/showdoc/RichardOBrien-1979Interview.php

"It was just completely perfect, just something he was born with": *The Guardian*, October 20, 2006

"There may have been other actors that I considered initially for the role of Frank": quoted in Michaels and Evans, *Rocky Horror from Concept to Cult*

"Perhaps Garbo's greatest screen role": Roger Baker, *Drag* (New York: New York University Press, 1994)

"The shoes were very important": *Time Out*, August 1973

"I thought the story sounded awful": 1979 interview with Patricia Morrisroe, http://www.rockymusic.org /showdoc/SueBlane-1979Interview.php

"The casting of Frank": *The Scotsman*, June 23, 2010

"It was a play": *JAM* Magazine, October 1979

"The element of transvestism wasn't intended as a major theme": 1979 interview with Patricia Morrisroe, http://www .rockymusic.org/showdoc/RichardOBrien-1979Interview .php

"There was one time I will never forget": Cocklenuggets. blogspot.com, September 26, 2010

"I auditioned for the play and": http://www.reviewgraveyard. com/2006_Interviews/06-05-22_PatriciaQuinn.htm

"Michael White coming up to me after the first night": 1979 interview with Patricia Morrisroe, http://www. rockymusic.org/showdoc/RichardOBrien-1979Interview. php

"Brian Thomson's blue-canvassed": The Inaugural Rex Cramphorn Memorial Lecture,

Belvoir Street Theatre, Sydney, July 23, 1995

"I could never imagine that at the time": *Evening Telegraph*, Peterborough, UK, January 18, 2011

"I think certain elements of punk": Michaels and Evans, *Rocky Horror from Concept to Cult*

"I never gave *Rocky Horror*": author interview, 1996

"When someone suggested we do *Rocky* as a film": 1979 interview with Patricia Morrisroe, http://www.rockymusic .org/showdoc/RichardOBrien-1979Interview.php

"I remember waking up one morning": 1979 interview with Patricia Morrisroe, http://www.rockymusic.org /showdoc/SueBlane-1979Interview.php

"When Lou Adler and Michael White": http://moviemikes .com/2010/04/interview-with-jim-sharman/, April 2010

"Insisting on staying with the original cast for Frank": http:// www.rockyhorror.com/history/21questions_sharman.php

"You know when I did": Movies Online, http://www .moviesonline.ca/movienews_13445.html

"One, I can't act": *People* Magazine, October 2000

"I never expected to be the object of a cult": *Shock Treatment* press release 1981

"The music for the film was re-arranged by Richard": http:// www.rockyhorror.com/history/21questions_sharman.php

"In the stage version, there are usherettes": http://
moviemikes.com/2010/11/interview-with-patricia-quinn/
November 2010

"Because the first 20 minutes": 1979 interview with Patricia
Morrisroe, http://www.rockymusic.org/showdoc/SueBlane
-1979Interview.php

"The version with 'Superheroes' is the original ending":
http://moviemikes.com/2010/04/interview-with-jim
-sharman/ April 2010

"The worst thing about the shoot was": *Hitfix*, September 2010

"The schedule was so tight that the film": http://moviemikes
.com/2010/04/interview-with-jim-sharman/, April 2010

"The movie had a lot of surprises and I didn't know":
http://moviemikes.com/2010/11/interview-with-patricia
-quinn/, November 2010

"One of the best things that ever happened to me was *Rocky
Horror*": quoted on http://quotedepot.net

"we all came out": Michaels and Evans, *Rocky Horror from
Concept to Cult*

"The film runs for 90 minutes": *The Scotsman*, June 23, 2010

"While I was in New York": 1979 interview with Patricia Morrisroe, http://www.rockymusic.org/showdoc/RichardOBrien
-1979Interview.php

"There's no reason to saturate it": Bill Henkin, *The Rocky
Horror Picture Show Book* (New York, Plume, 1979)

"Word of mouth was great": Cocklenuggets.blogspot.com, September 26, 2010

"after a strong initial release": http://www.rockyhorror.com/ history/21questions_sharman.php

"It was in the early days": http://moviemikes.com/2010/04/ interview-with-jim-sharman/ April 2010

"when I saw it downtown in New York": http://www.bullz-eye.com/television/interviews/2008/barry_bostwick. htm, August 2008

"I took Natalie": *Igby Goes Down* press release

"Well, when you do": Richard O'Brien, Celebrity Cafe.com, September 1, 1999

"The intentions of the two films": *Shock Treatment* press release

"As with *Rocky*, this film": http://www.rockyhorror.com/ shocktreatment/introduction.php

"What a waste of money": http://www.bullz-eye.com/ television/interviews/2008/barry_bostwick.htm, August 2008

"I've never danced": www.smh.com.au

"Jett never quite adapts": *Entertainment Weekly,* November 24, 2000

"We went back and forth": Brad Armstrong, *Adult Video News*, February 2011

BIBLIOGRAPHY

Baker, Roger. *Drag: A History of Female Impersonation in the Performing Arts.* New York: New York University Press, 1994.

Boot, Andy. *Fragments of Fear: An Illustrated History of British Horror Films.* London, Creation Books, 1996.

Harding, James. *The Rocky Horror Show Book 1973—1987.* London, Sidgwick & Jackson, 1987.

Henkin, Bill. *The Rocky Horror Picture Show Book.* New York City, Hawthorn/Dutton, 1979.

Medford, Howard. *Hammer House of Horror: Behind the Screams.* New York City, Overlook Press, 1996.

Michaels, Scott, and David Evans. *Rocky Horror: From Concept to Cult.* London, Sanctuary, 2000.

O'Brien, Richard. *The Rocky Horror Show Singalong.* London, Music Sales, 2007.

O'Brien, Richard, and Jim Sharman. *The Official* Rocky Horror Picture Show *Movie Novel*. New York City, A&W Visual Library, 1980.

Piro, Sal. *Creatures of the Night II: More of the* Rocky Horror Picture Show *Experience*. Detroit, Stabur Press, 1995.

———. *Creatures of the Night: The* Rocky Horror Picture Show *Experience*. {Add city:} Stabur Press, 1990.

Piro, Sal, and Michael Hess. *The Official* Rocky Horror Picture Show *Audience Par-tic-i-pation Guide*. Detroit, Stabur Press, 1991.

Rigby, Jonathan. *English Gothic: A Century of Horror Cinema*. London, Reynolds & Hearn, 2000.

Rock, Mick. *Rocky Horror*. Berlin, Schwarzkopf & Schwarzkopf, 2005.

Samuels, Stuart. *Midnight Movies*. New York City, Collier Books, 1983.

Tellote, J. P., ed. *The Cult Film Experience: Beyond All Reason*. Austin: University of Texas Press, 1991.

Thomson, Brian. Rocky Horror Show *Scrapbook*. London, Andre Deutsche Ltd., 1998.

———. *The* Rocky Horror Show *Book*. New York City, Star Fleet Productions, 1979.

Weinstock, Jeffrey. *The Rocky Horror Picture Show*. New York City, Wallflower Press, 2007.

Weinstock, Jeffrey Andrew. *Reading Rocky Horror:* The Rocky
  Horror Picture Show *and Popular Culture.* Basingstoke,
  Palgrave MacMillan, 2008.
www.rockymusic.org
www.rockyhorror.com

INDEX